Proven Option Spread Trading Strategies

by Billy Williams

1

Disclaimer

It should not be assumed that the methods, techniques, or
indicators presented in these products will be profitable or will
not result in net losses. Past results are not necessarily
indicative of future results. Examples presented here are for
educational purposes only. These examples are not
solicitations to buy or sell. The author, publisher, and all
affiliates assume no responsibility for your trading results.
There is a high risk in trading.

HYPOTHETICAL OR SIMULATED
PERFORMANCE RESULTS
HAVE CERTAIN INHERENT
LIMITATIONS. UNLIKE AN ACTUAL
PERFORMANCE RECORD, SIMULATED
RESULTS DO NOT
REPRESENT ACTUAL TRADING. ALSO,
SINCE THE TRADES
HAVE NOT ACTUALLY BEEN
EXECUTED, THE RESULTS MAY
HAVE UNDER- OR OVER-
COMPENSATED FOR THE IMPACT, IF
ANY, OF CERTAIN MARKET FACTORS,
SUCH AS LACK OF

What Others Are Saying

"Educated me tremendously! ...Everything was laid out in such a simple form that I was able to easily follow along. So far, I have profited over $300 in trades since starting this book. This may not seem like a lot but this is a great start considering I have never done this before." – Cassandra

"I have to say first that I know exactly zero about trading. I have been working on ways to generate income, and even though the market has been admittedly rough lately, I figured I could stand to learn something to be prepared when things started to pick up. This was a great place to start. The book is a logical step-by-step introduction to option trading. The author introduces key terms, and the in and out of trading. It is very thorough without getting mired in details. I certainly feel like I have a much better idea of what I could be doing financially to maximize my benefits. You can tell this is a very in depth approach (who ever said it superficial was reading another book, I think) by someone that certainly knows the subject." - Maege M.

"Overall it's a good lesson in how to review rank and buy stocks; its a great basic explanation of how to purchase options and how to assess stocks for option trading." – J. Crossland

"This is a very informative book. I never knew much about trading on the stock market, but this book is definitely a worthwhile resource. Before getting into how to buy, sell, and trade stocks, this book explains the terminology. Something that is extremely important if you wish to pursue

this venture. Once the terms have been explained, the author proceeds to talk about the different kinds of stocks available. I also like how this book tells you how to pick a stock to purchase and how you go about it. Basically this is Stock Trading 101 for people like me who know nothing about the stock market. Very easy to read and understand. A very good book and an invaluable resource." -McG

"I couldn't be more satisfied with this book. The author provides a professional and detailed approach to learning a solid foundation about option trading all provided by step-by-step methods and easy to understand writing. I decided to take a risk and buy this book when I saw that he had been published in the Future Magazine - I can now tell why because the content is amazing." – Manchester

"This is a no fluff book that gives you the hard facts about how to trade options successfully and a blueprint to do it. The book reinforces the basics to give you a strong foundation for option trading and actionable steps on how to apply them. Great addition to any beginner or veteran trader!" - Chris D.

Also by Billy Williams

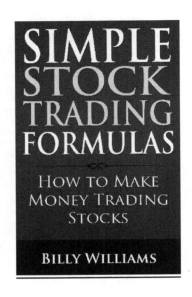

Simple Stock Trading Formulas

"How to Make Money Trading Stocks"

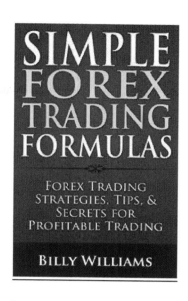

Simple Forex Trading Formulas

Forex Trading Strategie, Tips, & Secrets For Profitable Trading

Triple P Trading Course

Profitable Price Pattern Trading For The 21st Century Trader

To thank you for purchasing this book, I'd like to offer you a 47% + loyalty discount on my **Triple P Trading Course** offered through Udemy.com.

Use the coupon code "thanks4buyingposts" at the course's homepage to receive your loyalty discount at

https://www.udemy.com/triple-p-trading-course/.

Good Trading,

Billy W.
www.stockoptionsystem.com

Would you like to know where to find the strongest performing stocks?

Would you like to know the key factors that all winning stocks possess?

Do you think that having a simple step-by-step method for spotting winning stocks and avoiding the losers would add to your bottom line?

Grab my free report "How To Find Winning Stocks To Trade" at the url link below, enter your email address and I'll send you a free copy at no charge.

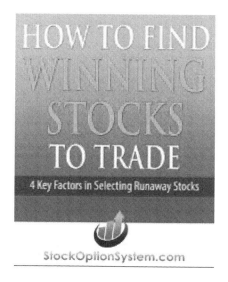

www.StockOptionSystem.com/posts

Table of Contents

1. Foreword

More than twenty years ago when I was first starting out as a trader, I remember picking up the latest copy of Futures Magazine. One of the articles read, "Pure directional option traders have great war stories about how they made a killing in the market but spread traders drive nicer cars."

At first, being a newbie, I didn't fully understand the wisdom of that statement, but as time went on and I grew in experience I finally got it.

If you love option trading or are thinking about option trading, there is nothing like the sheer thrill of catching a trend at the right time with options. I mean, what's not to love? Options have an enormous edge when it comes to leverage and limiting your risk to only the price of the option you're trading. If you time it right, you can make money hand over fist.

But the maddening thing about option trading that way is that sometimes you can do everything right but still lose money. Why? Because even though trading trends or breakouts with options are incredibly lucrative, volatility can sometimes work against you.

Though options have incredible leverage and risk control, if your timing is bad, your option can lose so much value by the time the move you predicted materializes that you end up at a loss anyway.

Add in commission costs and the spread between the bid/ask price and you've got a few hurdles to clear before you make any money.

So what edge do option spread traders have that helps them overcome some of these challenges?

Option buyers typically carry more risk than option sellers because options, also called derivatives, are "wasting assets," which means their value is tied to a definite period of time.

If you're long call options on a stock you think is going higher but trades sideways, or even declines in price, then your call option position is losing value, not just because the stock's price action is going nowhere, but also because time is also eating away at the value.

This is why stories of traders making a fortune with options are fairly common. When things align correctly, it's like winning a huge jackpot! Sadly, however, huge windfalls like this are typically followed by losing a fortune as well. If this rollercoaster ride doesn't sound appealing to you (and it doesn't to me either), then keep reading.

Spread traders use options to make the biggest weak link that common option traders face—time decay—work for them rather than against them. They do this by constructing low-risk option spread positions using proven option strategies combined with step-by-step trade setups. Used correctly, this places the odds in your favor, virtually locking in profits and helping you rack up a long string of winning trades.

Directional traders need price movement in order to profit, but option spread traders don't. If a stock trades flat, upwards, or even downwards, to a degree, then the spread trader can still come out ahead.

Those are three-to-one odds in your favor before you ever put on a spread trade, and you can increase those odds of success by using a proven system to help you select the best trades.

GOOG (Google)
Nov 11 2013 02:51:35

Price Avg 200 Avg 50 Avg 10

© FreeStockCharts.com

Courtesy of FreeStockChartes.com©. If you had bought a call option as Google moved higher in May of 2013, you would have gained a small profit when it reached the $920 level. However, if you decided to hang on because you thought it would go higher, you would have had to sit through a pullback and tread water while hoping the trend continued.

While you will miss out on some wildly successful and staggeringly profitable trades at times by trading only a pure call or put option, you will achieve a level of

14

consistent profitability and stability that few traders ever achieve by using option spreads.

These option trading strategies aren't difficult to learn, but they do require some patience and study.

If you're a "gunslinger-type" trader who trades for thrills and swings for the fences in every trade, this is not the strategy for you.

If you have no regard for risk control and believe that the markets are a giant casino where you can "bet on black," then these methods aren't going to match your personality.
If patience isn't a strong trait for you and you crave lots of trading transactions during the day, then you're going to be sorely disappointed with spread trading and it might be better for you to look for excitement elsewhere.

If you're still reading, you're probably wondering what you can expect.

First, let me share a few things with you.

If you've held stocks or mutual funds over the past ten to fifteen years, you've experienced one of the worst periods of stock market investment returns in history. When the stock market bubble popped in early 1999, it destroyed trillions of dollars of investors' capital and caused a ripple effect that would be felt by every investor across the globe for the next thirteen years.

GOOG (Google)
Nov 11 2013 12:00:00
Price Avg 200 Avg 50 Avg 10

© FreeStockCharts.com

Google Becomes Range Bound
For 4 Months

980.00
960.00
940.00
920.00
900.00
880.00
860.00
840.00
820.00
800.00
780.00
760.00

.pr
13
May   Jun   Jul   Aug   Sep   10/17/2013

Courtesy of FreeStockChartes.com©. Google went on to retest the $920 level but once again declined to its previous price low and found support. If you were holding Google call options then there is a good chance they were wasting away as time decay took effect.

In the last decade, give or take a year, the stock market has been stuck in a giant trading range that has seen stocks trade up and down like a giant seesaw and left investors with the impression that the game is rigged, the table is tilted, and the stock market is little more than a giant casino.

The buy & hold strategy that served so many generations of investors in gaining financial independence has left a big question mark in the hearts of Main Street as to whether it works anymore.

16

Now, many investors see the stock market as a giant casino that benefits only the insiders on Wall Street, and for good reason, which I'll get into in just a moment.

Since the dot-com era, another bubble has formed, this time in the housing industry, which came to a head in 2008 and almost took down the entire global financial system.

Investors again saw their investments take another big hit when it was just starting to see a glimmer of hope of recovering from massive losses nine years earlier.

As of this writing, investors in the U.S. are flocking to gold and silver as the Federal Reserve prints money around the clock, destroying the value of the dollar in the process. Anxiety among investors, especially those approaching retirement age, in increasing as the Fed monetizes our debt by printing more money to service the existing debt. They are creating more debt for you and I to pay back in order to pay the existing debt currently on the books.

If you think the U.S. is the only one taking this "nightmare pill," you should know that the debt crisis in Europe and the rest of the world isn't helping things.

Ireland, Spain, Greece, Italy, and other major industrialized European powers are an economic basket case. Many have borrowed money back and forth from each other in order to pay the debt owed to other partners in the European Union.

All of this says that economic mismanagement across the globe has left the stock market on shakier ground than ever, with the possibility of another crash more likely than ever before.

GOOG (Google)
Nov 11 2013 02:54:05
Price Avg 200 Avg 50 Avg 10

© FreeStockCharts.com

You Miss The Move

1,150.00
1,100.00
1,050.00
1,013.67
950.00
900.00
850.00
800.00

pr 13   May   Jun   Jul   Aug   Sep   Oct   02:54:05   Dec

Courtesy of FreeStockChartes.com©. In late October, almost four months after you bought Google call options, your expected move in the stock took place and the stock exploded higher. But after four months, how much of your call option's value was left? And would it still derive the same profit potential? More than likely it wouldn't, but using an option spread trade would have let you sleep better by locking in your gain without worrying about whether Google was going up or not. Successful spread trading is built on patient application, not hit-and-miss timing.

While gold and silver are good investments to have in any market condition, the fact is that most retirement couples or individuals are not going to be able to live off of precious metals. Why? Because they belong to "inefficient markets," which means that they can't just pick up the phone and buy and sell like you can with stocks in the stock market, which is part of an "efficient market" through a stock exchange.

Plus, you can't collect dividends or interest payments from them, so while they are good as a hedge against inflation or a falling dollar, they don't serve the long-term financial interests of their owners.

With ever-mounting problems surrounding the stock market and the poor track record of the investment professionals, people like you are seeking answers on how to achieve greater returns while controlling your risk.

The answer is that you're going to have to be involved to some degree in navigating your way through this mess in order to reach your financial goals.

No one, and I do mean *no one*, is going to care more about your money or your future than you.

The good news is that there are few strategies as successful or as versatile over the long haul as option spread trading.

If you're willing to put in some time and master the basics of trading option spread, you'll gain a skill that will make a lot of money for you over time.

If you're patient with the process and let the strategies do their work, you can potentially earn sizable returns over time, maybe even create a second income stream for yourself and your family.

Option spread trading requires study, discipline, a healthy respect for risk, a strong focus on reducing risk as much as possible, patience to allow the strategies to do their work, self-reliance, and a strong desire for consistent profits and higher returns.

If that strikes a chord with you, this is what you can do with option spread trading:

- Create your own "dividend" by selling the call options on a position and collecting the premium.

- Sell call options on your stocks over and over again unless they are called away.

- If the stock declines, you'll have a "buffer" in the form of the premium you collect to protect you from loss.

- Gain a distinct edge by being an option seller and letting time decay work for you.

- Put an option spread position into play and then buy it back if the option you sold becomes cheaper (your return is lower but your market exposure and risk is less).

- Potential to make 2% to 15% each month safely (sometimes more).

- Achieve returns that are steady and consistent.

- Reach your financial goals much faster.

- Retire much earlier.

- You can build a sizable part-time income from a few hundred dollars up to several thousand a month.

- Your rates of return turn over at a higher rate, allowing you to get greater benefit from the law of compounding.

- And much more.

Now let me say this again: there are no free lunches in this life, especially on Wall Street. There are risks with any kind of trading, even something like trading option spreads. But if you're aware of the risks and willing to work at managing things effectively in order to come out on the other end of the trade and be profitable, you can be successful.

If you have bought lots of books and courses to achieve financial independence and left them unread and collecting dust, please don't buy this book or get a refund now if you have already bought it. There is no sense in torturing yourself, so just be happy with what you have and where you are. There is no shame in it as long as you're not deluding yourself in the process.

But if you decide to take action, then in the coming chapters you'll get a focused education on what option spread trading is really about and learn:

- How to pick the best trades and in what markets.

- What tools you're going to need.

- Detail how simple the strategies are and how to use them.

- Simple tools to help you make your trade decisions.

- Which moving averages help you determine the trend.

- What simple indicators to use.

- How to know which option to sell so that you make the most money.

- How to know which option to trade to lower your risk and increase winning percentages.

- What to do if things don't go as planned (this is going to be your backup plan to keep you from suffering unnecessary losses).

- And a lot more.

Ready?

Then let's get to it.

Billy Williams
StockOptionSystem.com

2. Introduction - First Things First

If you decided to buy this options book, you probably already understand at least something about options. Even those who have traded options before would do well to review some of the basics I will cover in this section. As the saying goes, the difference between professionals and amateurs is that the professional always practices so they get it right every time, whereas the amateur practices to avoid getting it wrong.

By reviewing some of the basics of options we will be getting closer to the professional level of never getting our options trades wrong from a fundamentals perspective.

No one, even including my instructions in this guide, can offer you the promise that every options trade will be profitable. What I can offer you, through my instructions on your screen or paper, is a dramatic increase in the probability that you will have the knowledge and processes for creating higher-probability profitable options trades. So let's get started.

What are the advantages of options over, say, stocks, mutual funds, commodities, or a variety of other forms of investments?

Though there are many advantages of options, the main advantage is that we can take a small amount of money, control a large security or contract, and consequently create an outsized profit off of our small initial investment. In the investment world we call this ability granting leverage. Options leverage small sums of money to control larger amounts of money, which can result in very high profit percentages.

For example, let's take one of my favorite options markets to trade, the copper futures market. Now, trading copper futures as a commodity broker would mean taking on significant risk for large contracts of delivery of copper. Anyone who buys or sells a futures contract for copper actually has the responsibility of either taking on the delivery of the copper or providing delivery of the copper when that futures contract comes to term. Delivering or receiving a copper's futures contract is the equivalent of having four or five tractor-trailer loads of materials either delivered or shipped from your warehouse. That is not something I want to be involved in, nor is it something that most investors opt for.

For this reason, trading options on futures is a far better opportunity to get involved with the copper market while not creating the types of risks that futures trading might create. Going back to the basics, options are defined as the right but not the obligation to either purchase or sell the underlying security at a future date and at a certain strike price. The part to focus on is that this is a right but not an obligation. This means that we do not have to buy or sell exactly what the options contract says. The same thing applies whether we're dealing with copper futures or stocks or indexes for a variety of different securities when we buy them in options form.

We essentially get to ride the profit or potentially the loss of the underlying security controlled by the option, but we're not in the position of having to deal with buying or selling the underlying security if we do not want to.

Options are either calls or puts. I can sell a call or buy a call, sell a put or buy a put. Despite all the complex types of options trades I will write about in this guide, they really all come down to these four choices. The other terms popular in regard to options and futures and the market in general are going long and going short. Going long means we are bullish on the price of a security or an option going up. Bullish means essentially that we expect the price to increase. When we go short, we are expecting the price of either the security or the options on a security to go down. This is also known as being bearish.

Some people try to use call or put with the same type of meaning as going long or going short, but that can get very confusing. As much as possible, I will use simply call or put to describe the transactions and bullish or bearish, but not the terms long or short.

Options allow us to control the underlying security the option is based on with less money than it would normally take to buy the security directly.

Take, for example, the price of Google, GOOG, right now: $890. If we want to buy a hundred shares of Google, we have to spend $89,000 plus commission. Generally if I buy shares of stock, that means that I am bullish on the price of the stock or I expect the price of the stock to increase. If I do not happen to have $89,000 handy to go ahead and buy a hundred shares of Google, I can decide that I would like to control ten shares by buying options on the price of Google.

As I write this, I can buy a Google call option at around the strike price of $900 (these terms will be explained shortly) for about $124 per option. Doing the quick math on the price of each option, I discover that I can control a hundred shares of Google for $12,400. I will benefit when the price of Google goes off, and I can still create a fairly significant profit from the price of Google rising, but I do not have to come out of pocket $89,000 to buy ten shares of Google. I only need to come up with $12,400 plus commission, unless there are any margin requirements for taking on the option, which is unlikely in this case.

As you can see from the example, options allow us to control some expensive securities for not a lot of money.

Taking a closer look at my example, I will explain some of the terms I used earlier in describing the options purchase.

Underlying security: the security the option gives the right to (GOOG in the example)

Current price of GOOG: price of security determines when an option is in or not in the money ($887 in the example)

Strike price of option: the price point where the holder of an option can exercise the right to buy or sell the underlying security; sometimes called the exercise price ($900 in the example)

Expiration date of option: the date the option expires and becomes worthless (November 22, 2013 in the example)

Price of the option (this includes several factors discussed below): $124.00 (note that options are generally purchased in lots of a hundred shares), making the real purchase $12,400 for a hundred shares, but the point is the same, and some brokers allow mini-trades in the ten-share range

Type of option (for going long or being bullish on the price of GOOG): call

Side of trade: bought a call/long side.

I'm going to look at the price of the options in a little bit more detail to explain several factors. A lot of people will go into great depth doing theoretical calculations on the price of options, but that does not generally lead to great trading.

The price of an option includes four basic factors: time value, intrinsic value, option premium value, and the strange term "moneyness."

Because most of the readers of this guide have already traded options, I am going to cover these terms in the most basic fashion.

Moneyness refers to whether the option is in the money (ITM), at the money (ATM), or out of the money (OTM).

The following descriptions are for when we buy a call or a put.

For a call, when the strike price is below the price of the underlying security, the option is in the money. If the price of the underlying security is below the strike price of the call option, the option is out of the money. When the price of the underlying security matches the price of the strike price for the call option, the option is at the money.

For a put, when the strike price is below the price of the underlying security, the option is out of the money. When the strike price is at the price of the underlying security, the option is at the money. When the strike price is above the price of the underlying security, the option is in the money.

The option premium is the value placed on the option for the risk taken by the party selling you the option for providing the option.

The intrinsic value of the option relates to the mathematical value between the strike or exercise price and the underlying price of the security. In the example above, Google had risen to $910 before my call option expired, so the intrinsic value of my call option would simply be $910 - $900 = $10. Pretty simple stuff.

Time value makes up the last component of the price of an option. Time value is one of the most important aspects of options. Unlike owning a stock, when I own an option I have a limited time to exercise that option. Each day that goes by that I have not exercised the option, the time value of that option decreases. Time value can also include other aspects of options such as moneyness, but generally time value decreases as the exercise date for the option nears. The term for the decrease in the value of options as the exercise date nears is known as time decay.

That covers the basics of options. Taking a look at some of the advantages of options, they almost seem too good to be true.

1. Options give us leverage to control a larger security value than we otherwise would be able to with the same amount of funds.

2. Options allow us to limit our risk of exposure to the underlying security.

3. Options allow us to execute trades that have a high probability of turning a profit and a very limited risk of loss.

4. Options can protect our investments in the underlying security such as stocks, commodities, bonds, and mutual funds.

5. Options allow us to invest and trade in a wider range of assets that we may otherwise not be able to afford. This diversification can lead to more stable returns in a portfolio.

I am sure there are other advantages I have not included here. These are the major ones and certainly enough to entice most traders to engage in options trading.

With all this good news, there must be some bad news, right?

I have never seen uncontrollable disadvantages with trading options, otherwise I would not be an options trader, but I can understand that for some traders options are more complicated than they can deal with. Many investors will never go on the short side of investing or trading in their entire lives. When it comes to options trading, we all have to be comfortable on the short side, or selling calls and buying puts, in order to be successful options traders.

I might include the complexity and variety of options trades as being a disadvantage, but the fact is, we really only need a certain number of options trades and strategies in order to have enough tools to take advantage of the varieties of markets we are likely to encounter. That is what this guide is about: giving readers enough information that they can be confident with trading one of the safest forms of trading options: spread trading.

One major disadvantage of options that must be mentioned is that there is the potential to lose far more than you invest. This can only happen if you are in the position of selling an option.

Some brokers require that in order to trade options you have a certain number of years of experience in trading or a certain net worth, or that you have to have a certain value in your account. This is less about a disadvantage of trading options then it is simply the system of checks and balances in the financial brokerage world.

In a nutshell, there are many advantages and very few disadvantages to trading options.

Fortunately, we can trade options on almost anything that is a security. One of the requirements of most options is that the underlying security has sufficient volume for there to be a market for the options. Some smaller stocks and lightly traded months in commodities and some other indexes that are not popularly traded sometimes will not have options assigned to them. Even if they do have options available for them, as some examples in this guide will show, we will have to be careful about which months and strike prices we buy because we want enough volume for us to be able to buy and sell in the market without "being" the market.

When I first entered into the coppers futures market and wanted to buy options, they were somewhat hard to come by for the strike prices and months I wanted. I ended up having to buy options on a major copper stock, a mining company called Freeport-McMoran that served as a proxy for copper futures.

This demonstrates that there are many types of options. Options are available for most of the big board stocks listed on the New York Stock Exchange and the S&P 500 and many of the Wilshire stocks. Options are available on most commodities. And options are, of course, available on the major indexes such as the NASDAQ, the Dow Jones industrial average, and worldwide indexes.

In list form, the types of options we can work with include calls or puts on any of the following basic types of securities:

> 1. Stocks - GOOG, APPL, IBM, etc. and smaller capitalization stocks

2. Commodities - oil, gold, silver, cattle, corn, copper, etc.
3. Indices - DJIA, SP500, etc.
4. Mutual funds and ETFs - GLD, SLV, and many others.

Risk Identification with Options

When I buy a call or a put option, I have automatically limited my risk to the amount of money I paid for those options. However, when I sell a call or a put option, I have opened myself up to virtually unlimited risk. Even though this can be seen as too risky by some options traders, it also happens to be one of the best ways to make money with options. Options spread trading as discussed in this guide does require selling calls and puts frequently. The key to controlling the risk with selling calls and puts is proper trade setup, understanding the technicals of the underlying security, and understanding the risks of the trade from all angles. Our strategy, then, is to minimize the risk of each trade by protecting ourselves with the option spread strategies discussed in this guide.

Properly set up, selling options in the form of calls or puts can be a well-managed risk that generally leads to profitable trades.

One aspect of options trading that deals with the risks of options concerns the two terms known as assignment and exercising.

Exercising an option means just what we would expect: the person who holds the option decides to exercise it. This means if I sell a call to a buyer and the buyer decides to exercise the call, I then have to deliver the stock or the underlying security to the buyer as the option dictates.

Assignment refers to when the option is exercised by the option holder. The person or institution that wrote the option is said to be assigned to deliver on the terms of the options contract. According to the options clearinghouse, about 17% to 20% of options have been exercised historically. This means that almost one out of every five options could be exercised and then assigned.

To my complete surprise, I have never had an option exercised, and I have never had an option assigned on me. Part of the reason for my good luck at avoiding exercising and assignment is that I tend to trade options in the commodities market rather than in the stock market, and very often the other side of those trades has no interest in taking delivery on large futures contracts. If, however, you are trading in the stock market, assignment and exercise events are something that have to be considered in your trading setups.

Why This Guide Focuses On Advanced Options Strategies Called Option Spread Trading

The reason this guide focuses on options spread strategies instead of either just going long or short or just buying puts or calls is that option spread trading offers some of the best profit opportunities while minimizing losses. I have often wondered why all options traders do not use spread trading strategies. I believe the reason more options traders do not take advantage of options spread trading strategies is that they simply do not understand how to set them up and benefit from them. As soon as they understand the concepts and put some time into developing options spread strategies for themselves, they realize what a great opportunity they are. Generally speaking, options spread trading is using the purchase and sale of options of the same class more or less simultaneously on the same underlying security but choosing different expiration dates or a different strike price.

When I buy a call or put, what I am really doing is betting on the direction of the underlying security to go either up or down to generate a profit for me. When I decide to enter into an option spread trade, instead of being concerned about the direction of the underlying security going up or down, what I am more concerned about are the relationships between the two options I'm either buying or selling. I am less concerned about the underlying securities absolute price than I am about the relationship between the two options I am buying or selling. This will become more obvious as I dive into some of the details of options spread trading.

One of the great things about options spread trading is that even though I am engaging in double the number of trades compared to just a single options buy or sell, I am reducing my net cost of trading. Remember that discussion about the price of options and premiums? Instead of paying the premium cost of the price of the option, I am now receiving the premium cost because I'm selling the option that reduces my net cost of entering options trade. Now you understand one of the major benefits of options spread trading: you can get paid when you enter the trade, which is called getting credit.

Like most things in life, getting a credit and getting paid when we enter the trade means we have also entered into a risk relationship with the person who has purchased the option we sold. When I explain how options spread trading works, I'm sure you'll understand the details of this credit concept. For now it's just enough to understand that unlike simple buying a call or a put, in options spread trading we are actually getting a discount, or a net credit, for entering into the trade because we are on the other end selling a call or selling a put.

3. What is Option Trading?

As I discussed in the previous chapter, an option spread is when we simultaneously purchase and sell options of the same class on the same basic security but with different expiration dates or a different strike price.

With that possibly confusing definition in mind we are now going to take a look at examples of a real spread trade to clear up any complexity.

I will stick with the previous example when I was bullish on the price of Google.

In this case, instead of just buying a call option on Google at $900, I decide I'm going to engage in the same idea of the trade where I expect the price of Google to go higher, but this time I want to protect myself somewhat by engaging in a spread trade.

The strategy I will use is known as the bull call spread.

I am going to buy one in-the-money call option, and I'm going to sell one out-of-the-money call option.

In Chapter 3, where I explain a variety of options spread strategies, I will detail the thinking that goes into choosing a bull call spread. It is largely a way to take advantage of the price of an underlying asset going up moderately in the next few months.

In the case of this form of option spread I will actually be debited. With Google at around $887, the way this options trade will work is I will enter a bull call spread by buying a call that is already in the money, such as at $850 for the strike price, and then I will write a call for the same expiration date that is out of the money somewhere in the neighborhood of $910 or $920.

The in-the-money call will cost me approximately $55, while the out-of-the-money call will earn me about $18. My debit for entering this trade is $55 - $18 which equals $37. Keep in mind the multiply-by-a-hundred rule for options prices (note: I am keeping the numbers just as they appear in the options pricing chart for simplicity).

How I chose the expiration dates and strike prices and calls is not important at this point, but it is important for you understand what an option spread looks like, what some of the costs and benefits are, and why you would use them.

The advantage of this bull call spread over simply buying a call is that I have reduced my expense in buying a call by selling a call that is out of the money. The astute reader will notice that I have also reduced my potential upside on this investment relative to strictly buying a call option. This is an absolutely correct observation. However, the point is that I have also reduced my exposure and my risk. That is the name of the game with options spread trading. I want to reduce my risk and increase the likelihood of profit on every single trade.

Here is another example. What If I decide that the price of Google has risen too far too fast and I think it is ready to drop? This is a bearish stance, and I want to go short on Google options. The strategy I will use for this bearish stance is bear call spread. One of the nice aspects of the bear call spread is that it immediately puts money in my pocket—it could be putting money in your pocket soon as you enter the trade. In simple terms, I will buy one out-of-the-money call, and I will sell one in-the-money call.

Sirens may be going off in your mind when you see the idea of selling one in-the-money call. You might be asking yourself, "Can't the trader who buys the in-the-money-call immediately ask for exercising or assignment of the option?" The answer is yes, the person who buys the in-the-money call may decide to exercise or issue an assignment on the call, but they are paying for the option with the premium of its being in the money, so the likelihood of their immediately exercising the option is not very high, though it must be considered.

The expectation when entering this type of option spread trade is that the underlying security is on the way down so that the call expires worthless. This allows me to pocket the entire payment for selling the call.

Taking Google numbers as an example, with Google at $887, I decide to sell a November call at $870 for a price of $30, and I decide to buy a November call at a $900 strike price for $15. My net credit for entering this trade is $15. If as I have expected the price of Google drops to $850, say, then all of the options expire worthless and I get to keep the $15 credit. If, however,

I read the tea leaves regarding Google incorrectly and Google decides to take off for the moon, reaching a level of $950 before the expiration of the options, here is how the math will look:

Both calls will expire in the money with my November call at $900 having an intrinsic value of $50; the call I sold at an $870 strike price will have an intrinsic value of $80. The spread between these two options is a loss of $30, though I get to keep the $15 credit for entering the trade. My net loss will then be $15 on the trade.

These examples of a bullish and a bearish option spread trading strategy are designed to give an idea of both the limit of the profit potential and the limit to the downside that option spread trading can bring to the more advanced options trader.

By now, some of the advantages of option spread trading are probably apparent, namely the reduction of risk and the possibility of earning money when you enter a trade.

There is one major advantage of options spread trading that a lot of traders miss, especially if they are smaller or just starting out, but they can have a very significant impact on the direction of a market and on the success of option trading in general for each investor.

The secret of option spread trading is that an option trader becomes almost invisible to the market. If I decide to go long and buy a lot of calls on Google or copper futures or oil or anything else, it's very obvious to other traders in the market what I am doing. If, on the other hand, I decide that I want to enter into options trades that still give me long exposure or bullish exposure to the stock or commodity I am interested in, the market cannot detect it because I am essentially going both long and short in the same market.

I can also hedge positions with spread trades when I have the stock I am taking options on, or perhaps I already own a significant position in a commodity I want to take the options on. This allows me to maximize my profit and minimize my risk because the options are protecting against the market going off the path of my anticipated direction.

Another amazing advantage of trading option spreads is that I can now take positions in markets where I am not sure of the direction of the underlying security. In all of the examples I have cited so far, I thought either that the price of Google was going to go up or that it was going to go down. I took an options position aligned with that reasoning. With options spread trading, I do not have to make a call on whether or not the price of the underlying security or commodity I want to buy the options on is going to go up or down. I can simply decide to enter an option trade that will bring a profit so long as the price of the underlying security does not go up or down.

This concept would be almost entirely foreign to an options buyer who only knows about calls and puts but does not understand spread strategies.

The options spread strategies for a market I am not certain of the direction of are called neutral spread strategies.

Spread trades generally offer less volatility than picking one side or the other of a trade. When I enter the long side of a trade with calls, the volatility in that direction can be extreme. If I have decided to protect my position by entering a bull call spread instead, I at least have some protection on the other side of the trade and limit my losses relative to strictly going into a call option.

Another advantage of spread trading that can add up quickly is that I am no longer quite as concerned about how quickly my orders get filled, or as it is known in the industry, slippage. Depending on the market I'm trading, slippage can be pretty severe if there is not a lot of volume or there are not a lot of buyer's sellers. However, with spread trading I'm not quite as concerned about the exact price I enter each trade at because these are hedged with my other side of the spread trade. The other assumption is that both sides of the trade may incur similar levels of slippage, balancing each other out.

One of the best features of spread trades is that they do not create greater probabilities of losing in all cases. In certain cases spread trades will create greater odds of winning, but not in all cases.

This simply means that entering a spread trade will never really hurt you in terms of increasing the probability that you will lose. That alone should be enough reason to enter spread trades for almost all forms of option trading unless you have some fantastic analysis that allows you to dedicate yourself strictly to one side of the trade, and even then it's usually not a great idea.

While I am obviously positive about the benefits of option spread trading, I am not blind to some of the negatives or disadvantages. Options spread trades can involve higher commissions and generally will because you are adding an additional trade to the mix. However, if the premium of the price you receive for one side of your options spread trade is significant enough, the commissions become a non-issue. The other disadvantage of options spread trading is that you can lower your maximum profit if you put on credit options. You can also limit the amount of maximum profit if you have hedged your position, such as in a debit option trade. The other disadvantage is that you are often in a position where you need to hold options until expiration.

Last but not least, because of the doubling of options purchases and selling calls or puts we are exposed to the possibility of assignment or exercise, and that can be a bit nerve-racking. As I wrote earlier, this can happen about 17% to 20% of the time, making it something we really do need to factor in. There are markets that this is far less likely to happen in such as certain forms of commodity trading, but in the stock arena it is quite possible that somebody will demand the shares. This means that the option has been exercised. It is certainly a risk of dealing with options spread trading and something that each investor has to determine for themselves whether it is an acceptable risk.

Now that we have discussed the many advantages and a few disadvantages of options spread trading, the reader might be asking themselves, "Is this the kind of trading I want to be involved with because of some of the risks of an option being exercised or the commission expense or the additional complexity?"

It's confession time for me. This may help the reader make the decision and jump full steam into being primarily an options spread trader. Even though I have traded options, stocks, and commodities for nearly two decades now, I was hesitant to enter into options spread trading for a good part of my career. Part of this was simply the high commission structure that used to be prevalent in the options marketplace, which is no longer a factor. The real reason was that I thought that options spread trading was much more complicated than I wanted to get involved with, and I was also very hesitant to expose myself to selling calls or puts where there may be a virtually unlimited downside or I might be assigned or have an option exercised.

After studying options extensively and getting my feet wet on the long side and then on the short side, I soon realized that not spread trading was exposing me to a continued risk of lower-probability profit trades without proper hedging. I was essentially forced into spread trading for risk management purposes.

I could not be happier that I eventually learned the ropes of spread trading and learned that I did not need to master the multiple types of spread trades out there and get incredibly complicated to impress people at dinner parties. The reason I trade with options, and I suspect the reason anybody reading this eBook trades with options, is simply to make a good, consistent return on trading investments month after month, year after year, decade after decade. Options spread trading is one of the best vehicles for doing just that.

All I learned that I needed in my toolkit to be a strong options trader were the basic strategies for taking bullish or long-oriented positions on options, taking bearish or short-oriented positions on options, and taking neutral positions on options. Once the basic strategies are mastered and the basic terminology is learned, any options trader can adapt to all the varieties of options strategies with virtually no trouble at all.

Although there are an awful lot of option trading strategies out there and many different names for the strategies, I will show you the basic ones that a newer spread trader needs in order to handle themselves in virtually any kind of market. I will examine a few in detail so that the same basic principles can be applied to almost any type of options trade you might want to step up to. I could get really advanced if that were warranted, but that may not be the best way to make money in the market, and it certainly is a good way to increase your costs.

A couple of cautionary statements before I get into the details of specific strategies. As with almost any kind of investment, any of the money invested in options, or, for that matter, in the market in general, must be money that you can afford to lose. This warning goes double for the trades where we are selling the rights for a party to demand delivery of some security or certain amount of money from us. This includes selling calls and puts.

This means that not everybody should be engaging in options trading or, especially, options spread trading. If all I ever do is buy a call or a put, I am never exposing myself to unlimited risk. However, I am also exposing myself to more risk than is probably necessary. As long as the reader understands that these strategies are for minimizing risk but that no strategy other than staying out of the market can eliminate risk totally, we are all clear to proceed.

Those readers who have decided that the potential risk is too great for them may want to consider whether or not they should be trading in options at all. I believe that if a person has decided to trade in the options market, they really owe it to themselves to use options spread trading more often than not. This is because, as mentioned as one of the advantages options spread trading, it will, in general, reduce our risk of loss. Even more important than obtaining a profit is avoiding a loss. Options spread trading is a fantastic way to minimize potential losses.

4. Types of Option Spread Strategies

By now we have covered some of the very basics of what option spread trading is, so I am going to go into some detail on the many kinds of options spreads we can get involved with. Do not worry if it seems intimidating at first because of the huge number of trading strategies there are. I'm going to go ahead and break them all down into ones that we might use for a bullish approach or for a bearish approach or for neutral approaches. This will make it simple for almost anybody to choose which option strategy to use for the particular market they are involved in or the approach they are taking to the market.

Types of Spread Strategies

There are three basic types of spread strategies. Beyond these three types of basic spreads there are more complicated versions of spreads that include intermarket, exchange, and delivery spreads, or intercommodity or commodity spreads. I will explain what those more involved forms of spread trades are, but the key thing to know right now is that we do not need to use those types of spreads and would have to have significantly more analysis for each type of those trades without really gaining a tremendous advantage if we don't understand the markets extremely well in those trades. So for now I'm going to focus on explaining the basic option spread trades that we would use in a single market for a single security and forget about intermarket, intrasecurity, and cross-commodity spreads for a moment.

These basic strategies are known as the vertical spread, the horizontal spread, and the diagonal spread. These names come from the relationship between the strike price and the expiration date of all of the options involved in the particular trade.

865.00	GOOG7131116P00865000	11.90	0.00	12.80	13.60	15	41
870.00	GOOG131101P00870000	11.80	↑1.20	11.30	12.30	109	66
870.00	GOOG7131101P00870000	15.00	0.00	9.60	12.50	2	19
870.00	GOOG131108P00870000	12.71	↑1.31	12.60	13.80	5	1
870.00	GOOG7131108P00870000	25.10	0.00	11.30	14.20	1	1
870.00	GOOG131116P00870000	15.30	↑3.10	14.50	15.20	191	384
870.00	GOOG7131116P00870000	12.70	0.00	13.60	15.30	1	61
875.00	GOOG131101P00875000	13.75	↑2.45	13.20	13.80	25	59
875.00	GOOG7131101P00875000	14.40	↑...	14.70	11.40	0	5

Courtesy of Google, Inc. ©. This is how an option price chart looks for GOOG for the November puts in the $865 to $875 range. This is a different date range from some of the other GOOG pricing examples.

If you are familiar with how options are priced online then you know that you go up and down vertically to find a differently priced option, whether that is a call or a put. Surprise! This is the basis for a vertical spread. The vertical spread refers to moving up or down vertically to find a differently priced option in the same expiration month and the same underlying security.

Horizontal spreads naturally refer to moving along the expiration date at the same price level.

Most of you have probably already guessed by now that a diagonal spread refers to moving along both the strike price and the expiration date, hence the name diagonal spread.

Very often, option prices will have the calls on one side of the strike price and the puts on the other. So for the image above, if I bought an $865 put and sold an $875 put, I would have engaged in a vertical spread.

For horizontal spread I would've bought an $875 November put and perhaps sold a $865 December put. The horizontal part of that trade comes from moving from November to December or any other month past November.

The diagonal trade would be simply buying an $865 November put and perhaps selling an $875 December put or buying an $875 December call or selling an $865 November put. Whether I buy or sell the put or call is not the important aspect. The important aspect is that I have crossed into a new month and I have selected a new price. This makes for a diagonal spread trade.

More often than not, options spread strategies are known by more specific terms than simply vertical, horizontal, or diagonal spread trades. They are known by terms such as bull calendar spread, collar, diagonal bull call spread, strangle, condor, and a host of other strange-sounding names.

Intermarket/exchange spread trading options across different exchanges are known as "intermarket option trading."

This can also be a form of arbitrage where we have detected a price discrepancy across different markets. This is really beyond the scope of this guide and is a form of trading that could fill an entire book on its own. Intermarket and delivery spread trading are trades that I am focusing on here because they are somewhat simpler to execute and rely on keeping things focused on a particular security and changing either the strike price or the exercise date.

Intercommodity option spread trading is exactly what it sounds like. Someone may decide to buy a natural gas future and sell a crude oil future or, for that matter, buy natural gas option on futures and sell crude oil options on futures. Making those kinds of trades means that I suddenly have to become an expert in two separate markets while I have also added a great deal of complexity to the pricing of the options. Any of the tools and strategies I discuss here can be applied to these different kinds of trades; it's just that to keep things simple, I will not get involved with cross-market, cross-commodity, or cross-exchange trades.

(Note: Only the low-risk options spread strategies will be chosen for full explanations and detailed guidance for use. The high-risk strategies are only being explained for completeness, not as a recommended strategy.)

Now I get to give you all the fancy names for all the different types of options I get involved with and that anybody reading this guide can decide to get involved with. Keep in mind that it's sort of like how a fighter might know how to do a jump spinning back kick and deliver a flying spinning elbow but the chances of them using anything beyond a jab and uppercut, a punch straight to the knees, and occasionally a shin kick are reasonably slim. Even better, the basics are usually more than enough to get the job done. I still want to give you the choice of which options to use when. I will give you the background on these different options and when they should be applied.

1) Butterfly Spread

With the butterfly spread I am approaching the market with a neutral strategy. I am not sure which direction things are going to go.

I buy one in-the-money call. I sell two at-the-money call. I buy one out-of-the-money call.

I can also construct something called a long-call butterfly that is similar to the standard butterfly. I expect the underlying stock or security not to move much before the options expire. For the long-call butterfly, I buy one lower in-the-money call, write two at-the-money calls, and buy an out-of-the-money call at a higher strike price. The most money I can make from a butterfly spread of this nature is when the underlying stock price doesn't do much of anything before expiring. This means that the lower strike calls expire in the money. I get to pocket that premium.

This is a limited risk strategy. The loss is more or less limited to the initial cost to enter the trade plus the commissions.

2) Calendar Straddle

Before explaining a calendar straddle, I need to explain what an option straddle is in general, which is also referred to as a long straddle. An option straddle is a neutral strategy that involves buying a put and a call at the same time for the same security, both at the same striking price and expiration date. The benefits of long straddles are that they are unlimited profit and they have a limited risk. That sounds like the kind of strategy I like to be involved with! Straddles, or long straddles as they are often known, are the type of strategy I will use when I expect significant changes in price in the short term. All I need to do is buy one at-the-money call and buy one at-the-money put.

The magic thing about a straddle is that whether the price moves downward quickly or upward quickly, there is unlimited profit potential. The only downside to a straddle of this nature is that if the underlying security does not move much in either direction and settles at the money, then I have just lost my investment in the options. To recap, I have unlimited profit potential no matter which way the stock moves, as long as it moves considerably from the at-the-money price, and I have limited risk because all I can lose is the amount of money I invested in the options.

Now that I have explained what a straddle is, I can go ahead and give you the details on another form of straddle called a calendar straddle.

The calendar straddle sells a near-term straddle and buys a long-term straddle. The reason I would do this is because I will profit from the time decay of the near-term options sold under the expectation that there will be very little movement in the underlying security for the options in the near term. The key thing to understand is that a long straddle, or any straddle generally, should be used when you expect a lot of movement or volatility in the underlying security, whereas a calendar straddle is for just the opposite situation. I am expecting very little movement with the underlying security or the market. I want to benefit by the time decay of the option and make that a big part of my profit.

The complete opposite of the general straddle or long straddle, the calendar straddle anticipates that the underlying securities are not going to move much and are going to be trading at the strike price of the options I sold. At that price, both of the options I wrote are going to expire worthless allowing me to earn the money from selling those options. The longer-term straddle that I'm going to hold suffers a small loss because of the time decay.

Calendar straddle is a limited profit and limited loss or limited risk strategy.

3) Condor

Using the word condor just makes me feel cooler when I am talking about this trade at a party. Condor is considered one of the more advanced trading strategies, and in my opinion it is not all that necessary to have in our toolkit. I will explain it for completeness, however. I will sell one in-the-money call. I will buy one in-the-money call at a lower strike price. I will buy one out-of-the-money call also at a higher strike price, and then I will sell one out-of-the-money call at a lower strike price.

All of these calls are options expiring in the same month. There are a wide variety of condors, including long condor and short condor, where you steer the trade slightly to gain more profit if there is a small upward trend in the market or a small tower trend in the market. However, the basics remain the same.

If the underlying security price happens to lodge between the two middle strike prices at the expiration, then I have gained the maximum profit. The most I can lose with a condor is what I have paid in premium and the commission. This situation will happen if the underlying security happens to go below the lowest strike price or if it goes above the highest strike price of any of the options involved. In short, I enter the condor expecting not a lot of volatility, and if I get a lot of volatility, that will create my loss.

4) Iron Butterfly

Like the general butterfly spread, the iron butterfly is for a low-movement underlying security where I would expect the security to more or less stay put up to the expiration of the options.

I'd buy one out-of-the-money put, sell one at-the-money-put, sell another at-the-money call, and buy an out-of-the-money call. My objective would be that all of the options expire worthless and the credit I get by selling the at-the-money put and selling the at-the-money call goes right into my pocket. I did get a credit where I get paid to enter this trade. And that's as much money as I can possibly make with an iron butterfly. The limited risk for the iron butterfly happens much like the other butterfly spread where if the underlying security moves either at or below the strike price of the put purchased or the call purchased, then I lose.

5) Iron Condor

Similar to the basic condor, an iron condor is limited risk and is generally a non-directional trading strategy where you get a really good chance of just a small profit when the underlying security is once again not going anywhere price-wise.

I will sell one out-of-the-money put. I will also sell one out-of-the-money call. I will buy one out-of-the-money put at a lower strike price, and I will buy one out-of-the-money call at a higher strike price. One of the nice aspects of a lot of these condor spread trades is getting that credit to my account for selling the out-of-the-money put and the out-of-the-money call. The most I can earn is the credit I received when I enter the trade. I get paid up-front. Now the most I can lose is greater than the most I can earn. This is a disadvantage of the iron condor. If the stock price falls below the put or goes above the call, and also if it matches either the put or the call, then the maximum loss is going to be the difference between the strike price of the calls or puts less the credit received when I entered the trade.

In my experience there are not a lot of good reasons to use the iron condor.

6. Long Put Butterfly

Another low-volatility or low-movement trade is the long put butterfly. Here again I think that the underlying security is not going to move much either higher or lower by expiration. I am going to buy one out-of-the-money put. I'm going to sell at-the-money puts, and I'm going to buy one in-the-money put. As a reminder, buying an out-of-the-money put is buying a put with a strike price below the current security price. At-the-money puts have the strike price at the same price of the underlying security. An in-the-money put has a strike price above the current price of the security. This is just a refresher of out-of-the-money, at-the-money, and in-the-money references.

The limited profit is attained when the underlying security does not go anywhere. When this happens, the striking price of the highest put expires in the money. That's the one put I bought that was in the money.

The most I can lose for long put butterfly is the initial amount taken to enter the trade plus commissions. For this reason, it is kind of a strange trade because you take your loss up-front but are looking for a gain in the future. There are many trades commonly called credit spreads where you get your profit up-front, and if there is going to be any loss, it occurs in the future. That seems to me to be a better way to approach most trades.

7) Long Straddle

I already covered what a long straddle or a straddle in general is. I can let out the secret right now that a long straddle or a straddle is one of my favorite option trading strategies. The reason is fairly obvious. A long straddle provides for unlimited profit potential and very limited risk. If, as is often the case these days, I am trading in a market where there is a great deal of volatility, I will enter into a straddle or, specifically, a long straddle.

The long straddle once again is buying one at-the-money call and buying one at-the-money put, with the expectation that the underlying security is going to go significantly outside of the at-the-money strike price one way or the other. This means that either the put or the call will expire worthless but the other side will then have unlimited profit potential.

8) Long Strangle

This is sometimes known as simply a strangle. It is another neutral trading strategy. One of the beautiful aspects of a neutral trading strategy is that it allows us to trade when we really do not have a good idea of what the market is going to do. I happen to enjoy technical analysis, and I generally come down on either a bearish or bullish side, so I do not use neutral trading strategies with as much regularity as I use directional trading strategies. However, this does not mean that the reader may not choose neutral trading strategies until they have decided they have a firm grasp on the technical read of the market.

A long strangle is simply buying one out-of-the-money call and buying one out-of-the-money put. This allows us to have limited risk with the potential to make unlimited profit. This is much like a straddle. I am expecting a great deal of volatility in the near term when I enter either a strangle or a straddle. This happens to be one of those trades where there is a debit to enter the trade because I am buying both a call and a put. Fortunately, buying an out-of-the-money call and buying an out-of-the-money put is generally executed at a great deal of discount versus buying in the money or at the money, such as with a normal straddle. The most I can lose is when the underlying security falls between the two strike prices of those options I have purchased. Both options expire worthless and I lose the prices I paid plus the commissions for those options. However, if the underlying security moves outside of those options then the profit potential is virtually unlimited.

9) Neutral Calendar Spread

The neutral calendar spread is for when I am neutral toward the market in the short term for the underlying security the option is based on. My plan is to make my money and profit from the rapid dying of the near-term option because of time decay.

As the name suggests, the spread is based on calendar dates of the same security at the same prices. I will sell one near-term at-the-money call, and I will buy one long-term at-the-money call.

As with many spread trades, my profit is limited to the premiums I collect when I sell the near-term option, less the time decay of the other longer-term option. The most I can make is what I make at the beginning of the trade on entering it.

The downside risk or loss risk occurs if the stock price or security price the option is based on goes down and stays down until the exercise date of the longer-term option. The total amount I can lose is the payment it took to put on the spread.

With limited profit potential and limited loss potential, this is one of those trades that are good for small gains only.

10) Put Ratio Spread

Another neutral strategy, I will buy one in-the-money put, and I will sell two out-of-the-money puts. As crazy as it sounds, I have just exposed myself to an unlimited risk with a limited profit. With so many other ways to trade a neutral or non-volatile market, this is obviously not one of the better ones to expose myself to unlimited risk while limiting my profit.

The most I can make from a put ratio spread is when stock or the security price expires at the strike price of the options I have sold. The reason this is called a ratio spread in a put ratio spread is that I am dealing only with puts, and I have sold two more puts than I bought. Obviously, I could decide to sell three or four puts, or I could buy two puts and sell one put. This does trade differently than the two-to-one ratio, and the two-to-one ratio is one of the more common forms of the put ratio spread. The intrinsic value of the long put with either the addition or the subtraction of the credit or the debit of the spread is the maximum profit I can make on this trade.

On the dark side of this trade, if the underlying security nosedives and goes below my breakeven point at expiration, there is absolutely no limit to how much I can lose with a put ratio spread. My strong advice at this point is to forget I even mentioned a put ratio spread. The goal of this book is to introduce limited risk and highly profitable trades. My goal is not to introduce you to new, interesting-sounding option trades that can lose you all of your money while not having an unlimited upside.

11) Ratio Call Write

This form of option spread trade is a bit of an oddball for most traders. The reason the ratio call right is a strange trade is that I would have to own the underlying stock and then sell far more calls on that stock than I own. Once again I enter a crazy world where I have created a limited profit potential and unlimited risk. No thank you. To give an example of how this sort of trade would work, I would go long on a hundred shares of Google. Then I might sell two or three or five or ten at-the-money calls for Google. I am then hanging in the wind for the remaining shares of Google if the person who purchases the calls decides to exercise them.

In this case, a two-to-one ratio is simply two at-the-money calls for a hundred shares I might own. Keep in mind that in the terminology of options, if I'm buying an option, then it is referring to a hundred shares generally. For the sake of smaller numbers and clarity, in this book I often treat the options as just the price that is written on the options sheet, but those prices are usually multiplied by a hundred when you actually transact. This is not always the case, as there are situations and brokers that let you trade mini options. You can trade binary options and you can trade a variety of options that don't have a multiplication by one hundred, so it keeps it simpler for me to use the one price that is shown on the screen as the options quote.

The ratio call write is another option to run to the hills from.

12) Ratio Put Write

This is another option strategy to forget I even mentioned. However, for the sake of completeness I feel it is necessary to include some of these stranger and riskier strategies.

This strategy has limited profit potential and unlimited risk. This type of the trade happens if I expect that there will not be much movement in the underlying security the options are written on. I will short a hundred shares of the security and then sell two at-the-money puts. I consider this to be even worse than the ratio call write because not only am I selling puts, I'm also short a hundred shares of stock. This is a great way to get your neck wrung quickly.

My maximum and only real profit is the sale of the two at-the-money puts minus the commissions I'm paying.

The risk is completely unlimited because if the stock happens to drop below the price of the puts I sold, I am on the hook no matter how far down it goes. Not only that, but I am also on the hook if the price goes above that transaction.

I cannot think of any good reason to get involved with a ratio put write trade.

13) Ratio Spread

Ratio spread trade might involve buying one in-the-money call and selling two out-of-the-money calls. Or I could buy two in-the-money calls and sell three or five out-of-the-money calls. This is how it gets the name ratio spread trade. It is a generally neutral strategy where my expectation is that the underlying security will not move up or down much in the near term to the expiration of the options. A call ratio spread would use a two-to-one call ratio by buying calls at a lower strike price and selling two times the number of calls at a higher exercise or strike price.

The limit of ratio spread trades is when the maximum profit that can be gained is made when the security the options are priced on at expiration is at the strike price of the options sold. Both of the written calls will become completely worthless, and though I collect the premiums, the long call will make money when it expires in the money.

The danger and unlimited risk occurs if the security price rockets to the upside beyond my breakeven point. Then there is absolutely no limit to how much I can lose because I have to come up with the shares or the funds for the two out-of-the-money calls I sold.

The positive side of a call ratio spread is that there is little or no risk if the underlying security price takes a nosedive and drops. That is about all the advantage this particular trade has. It is a good trade to enter if the market has either a downward or a neutral bias. However, if there is a chance that there may be a leap to the upside for some particular reason, this is not the right trade to play around with.

14) Short Butterfly

The short butterfly is a good spread trade to keep in your back pocket for situations where the expectation is that there will be a lot of volatility in the underlying security. I set up a short butterfly trade by selling one in-the-money call. I sell one out-of-the-money call. I then buy two at-the-money calls. I need to select three strike or exercise prices for the short butterfly. There are two ways to maximize the profit with a short butterfly. Either the underlying security price goes higher than the higher strike price or it goes below the lower strike price and expiration.

The most I can make with the short butterfly is essentially the premium I receive for selling the one in-the-money call and the one out-of-the-money call less the commissions I have to pay for the entire transaction. If, however, the stock price does not move for the underlying security I'm buying the options on, then only the lower strike and call that was shorted expires in the money. I have to buy back that call and pay for its intrinsic value. This does limit my risk, but I also have limited upside potential.

15) Short Condor

This particular strategy has the advantage of being a limited risk strategy, though it is also a limited profit trading strategy designed to earn money when high volatility is expected. Unlike so many of the spread trades I have mentioned before that are focused on neutral markets where I do not have a perspective on whether the market is going to move with great volatility, with a short condor I expect there to be a significant move one way or the other. A short condor requires selling one out-of-the-money call at a higher strike price, buying one out-of-the-money call, selling one in-the-money call at a lower strike price, and buying one in-the-money call.

There are four steps or legs in this trade. One of the nice things about a short condor is that I earn my maximum possible profit when I enter the trade because it is composed of the premiums and a credit received for selling the two calls. If the underlying security stays between the strike prices of the lower long call and the lower short call, then I have incurred my maximum loss.

This type of a trade is good for markets where there is tremendous volatility in the underlying security. And by tightening up the expiration dates on the options I might buy, the chances of the options moving outside of the two middle strike prices becomes very high. This allows me to earn my maximum profit when I enter the trade and not have to be all that concerned that there will not be enough volatility to carry my profit through the expiration of the options.

16) Short Put Butterfly

The short put butterfly is for another situation where I expect there to be a lot of movement in the underlying security. Once again, it is a limited profit and limited risk strategy that is generally really good news. There are three strike prices I have to be concerned with. These are when I sell one in-the-money put, when I buy two at-the-money puts, and when I sell one out-of-the-money put. I get a net credit to enter this trade. So what I am looking for is for the underlying security to move outside of the trade zone for the strike prices of the puts I have entered into. This will give me my maximum profit, which is what I earn by selling the in-the-money put and out-of-the-money put less the commissions I had to pay for the entire transaction. If the stock or security for the option stays put, I know what my downside is. I have to deal with a downside limit that is actually higher than my profit potential. If the underlying security stays put and the price does not change, then the out-of-the-money put I sold I have to buy back at a loss for the entire trade.

The short put butterfly is a very reasonable spread trade, and one that is very good for markets where there is an expectation of significant movement one way or the other in the underlying security

17) Short (Naked) Straddle

This trade has me selling one at-the-money call and one at-the-money put of the same security at the same strike price with the same expiration date.

The word "naked" in this description about a naked straddle should set off alarms. The short straddle has unlimited risk because it involves selling a call and selling puts that are both at the money. This means that one way or another I will have to make up for one of these becoming in the money unless the underlying security does not move at all.

The most profit I can make with this trade occurs when the underlying commodity or underlying security price is at the strike price or the exercise price of the options I sold. If, however, the underlying security has moved up above that strike price or below that strike price, I am on the hook.

The profit is limited to essentially the premiums received less the commission, and the risk is unlimited. This is another one of those spread trades to forget about getting involved in.

18) Short Strangle

For a short strangle, or sell strangle, as it is sometimes called, I will sell one out-of-the-money call and one out-of-the-money put. As the reader is probably aware by now, whenever I sell a call or a put, even if they are out of the money I have opened myself up to unlimited risk. I will be opening myself to unlimited risk with a short strangle and limited profit. About the only positive thing that can be said about a short strangle is that when I enter it, because I have sold a call and a put, I get to keep those premiums. For this reason it is called a credit spread.

19) Variable Ratio Write

The variable ratio write is much like the ratio write strategy where the options trader has the underlying stock and decides to sell more calls than the number of shares they might own. It is another lousy idea for a trade. It has limited profit and unlimited risk, which is almost always a bad idea. The concept behind it is that I am expecting there to be very little movement in the near term of the underlying shares for the option. If I were foolish enough to enter this trade, I would have to be long, for example, a hundred shares, and then I might sell one in-the-money call and one out-of-the-money call. The reason it is called a variable ratio write is that I am writing one out-of-the-money call and one in-the-money call. This has a lower profit potential, but the area where I profit is wider because of the difference between the in-the-money and out-of-the-money calls. If at expiration the underlying security price is anywhere between the exercise or strike price of the two options I sold, then I have earned my maximum profit. The unlimited risk occurs if the underlying security moves outside the bounds of the two calls I sold. If the security ends up above the strike price of the higher strike short call or it ends up below the lower strike price of the short call, I lose money.

I label these types of trades IWLM—"I want to lose money"—trades.

20) Reverse Iron Condor

Unlike some of the trades recently discussed, the reverse or short iron condor does not expose us to unlimited risk. It exposes us only to limited profit, unfortunately. I either want limited risk or will accept limited profit, or limited risk with unlimited profit. But I will never accept, and recommend that no trader ever accepts, limited profit and unlimited risk.

The reverse iron condor gives us a reasonable level of risk and profit. The way to build a reverse iron condor is to buy one out-of-the-money put, buy one out-of-the-money call, sell one out-of-the-money put at a lower strike price, and sell one out-of-the-money call at a higher strike price. Even though I am selling a put and a call, there is generally a net debit for a cost to enter this trade. The maximum profit I can make with a reverse iron condor is limited to when the underlying security goes below the strike price of the short put or goes at the money or equal to a higher strike price of the short call. So what I'm looking for is a move outside the bounds of a short put or call. I take the loss when I enter the trade with the option premiums and expect to make up for it by exercising the trade at a profit.

21) Reverse Iron Butterfly

The word reverse means, in general, options trading, so this is either the reverse iron butterfly or the short iron butterfly. My expectation for profit with this type of trade is when the underlying security is going to make a very fast move either to the upside or to the downside. Again, what I am looking for is volatility. I create a reverse iron butterfly by selling an out-of-the-money put, buying an at-the-money put, buying an at-the-money call, and selling an out-of-the-money call.

This trade does cost money to enter because the premiums on the at-the-money put and the at-the-money call will be higher than the premiums I gain for selling the out-of-the-money put and the out-of-the-money call.

The most I can make with a reverse iron butterfly is when the underlying security price either drops below the strike price of the short put option or goes way over or equal to the strike price of the short call option. If either of those things happens, the difference between the calls and the puts minus the debit I took on to enter the trade is my profit. I lose the most if the underlying security does absolutely nothing, and that is limited to what I put in to enter the overall trade.

22) Long Guts

Finally, I get to explain one of my favorite option trades. Not only do long guts have a great name (who does not want to use long guts?), but it also has a characteristic that all of us should want, and that is unlimited profit and limited risk. I would enter a long guts trade when I think that the underlying security is going to have a lot of movement in the near term before my options expire. This is a debit type of spread because it does cost money to enter this trade.

I simply buy one in-the-money call, and I buy one in-the-money put.

If the underlying security either goes way above the strike price or way below the strike price of either the call or the put, then I have unlimited profit. The most I can lose is when the underlying security does not do very much and stays within the range of the call and put. In this case, both options will expire worthless, and my maximum loss is defined by what it cost me to enter the trade. All in all, this is a fantastic trade to use for highly volatile markets.

23. Short Guts

Even though short guts sound very similar to long guts, this is an entirely different trade and one I recommend avoiding. Short guts have the terrible quality of limited profit and unlimited risk. The unlimited risk comes from having to sell one in-the-money call and one in-the-money put. How much worse can it get than selling an option that is already in the profit for the person who's buying it?

Though I do earn a credit when I enter this trade, that is the most profit I can earn. However, if the price either goes below the already in-the-money put or above the already in-the-money call, there is an unlimited risk regarding how much I can lose. You have probably already guessed that this is a trade to forget about and avoid.

24. Long Call Ladder

The long call ladder is also occasionally referred to as the bull call ladder and is both limited profit and unlimited risk. This is another trade where I would expect little volatility in the underlying security prior to the expiration of the options. I buy one in-the-money call, sell one at-the-money call, and sell one out-of-the-money call. As I hope most readers have picked up on already, whenever I sell a call or a put, I am exposing myself to unlimited risk. This is okay if I am counterbalancing it with buying a call or buying a put. However, in this case, I am going on the long side of the trade. The most I can gain is when the underlying security is somewhere between the strike prices of the call options I have sold and the long call ends up being worth more than a short call, and that is how I get to make my profit. There is an unlimited risk to the upside. If the stock price or the underlying security price goes dramatically higher beyond the upper breakeven point or the upper call, then there is no limit to how much I can lose.

Put the long call ladder/bull call ladder on your avoid list.

25) Short Call Ladder

The short call ladder is far superior to the long call ladder. This is an unlimited profit and limited risk way of trading options that involves a pretty simple format of selling one in-the-money call, buying one at-the-money call, and buying one out-of-the-money call. This is for the type of environment where I might expect to see a lot of movement before the options expire in the underlying security. If the underlying security price goes down, then the long and short calls both end up being worthless. But if the underlying security ends up going up much higher, there is an unlimited profit potential because of the extra long call. The losses are limited on a short call ladder when the underlying security price is between the strike prices of the long calls on expiration. A higher long call will be worthless, but the lower striking long call is worth much less than the short call, so it results in somewhat of a loss but with very limited risk.

26) Long Put Ladder

This is another limited profit and unlimited risk type of trade that I am simply explaining so that you understand the terms. It is not a trade to enter into. I would have to buy one in-the-money put, and I would sell one at-the-money put and one out-of-the-money put.

This is another low volatility trade where I would make my money up-front when I sell the put options. However, if the price of the underlying security goes hard to the downside, my losses are virtually unlimited because of the puts I have sold.

With both limited profit and unlimited risk, this goes on the "please do not bother me with this trade" list.

27) Short Put Ladder

This type of trade has the great qualities of unlimited profit and limited risk. As with the other types of trades where I'm expecting significant volatility, I make the most money when the underlying security moves out of the near-term trading range I buy the options at.

To enter this trade, I would sell one in-the-money put, buy one at-the-money put, and buy one out-of-the-money put. This is all on the same underlying security and expiration date. If the stock or security price goes above my upside breakeven point for the puts, I am limited to the amount I earned from the initial credit when I sold my in-the-money puts. However, if the underlying security takes a nosedive to the downside, I have unlimited profit potential because of the two puts I purchased.

The short put ladder is a good trade to get involved in when you suspect that there is a downward bias to the market but you can't rule out an upward move because the upward move has limited risk for you. The downward bias you are expecting has unlimited profit potential.

28) Strip

The strip is a good strategy to know. It has unlimited profit potential and limited risk and is used if I think that the underlying security is going to do a lot of moving about in the near term but is much more likely to go down instead of up.

All I do to enter a strip is buy one at-the-money call and two at-the-money puts. The unlimited profit potential comes when the underlying security price moves either way up or way down before expiration, but I make more money if it goes with a downward move.

A strip can be constructed with any ratio the trader prefers. With a two-to-one put ratio to call, the downside move gets preference. I could decide to change that around and give the call preference.

The only risk of the strip is that the underlying security might be trading at the strike price of the call input options that were purchased. At that price, all the options end up expiring worthless. However, if we choose our expiration date and our underlying security correctly, there is a high probability for seeing significant profits with a limited risk.

29) Strap

A strap is another good trade with unlimited profit potential and limited risk. It is used if I think that the underlying security is going to have a lot of movement in the near term and is more than likely going to go up instead of going down.

I would enter with two at-the-money calls and then buy one at-the-money put. The unlimited profit potential occurs when the underlying security goes strongly in either the upward or downward direction at expiration, though I make more money with an upward move. The maximum I can lose is when the underlying security price at expiration is at the strike price of the call and the put options I bought so they expire essentially worthless. All I end up losing is the premiums I put in and the commissions for entering the trade.

There are many more option strategies I could have delved into and explained, but there is really no need to. The goal of this guide is to give you a small set of option spread trades you can use in a variety of conditions. Once you have developed a familiarity with option spread trading, you can go on to trade virtually any format of options in as sophisticated a manner as you want, and it will all feel relatively similar to you because they are built on the same principles.

This section is not intended to make anybody an expert in these particular strategies. The only intention of is to give you a brief understanding of how risk is set out in option spread trading. We learned, for example, that whenever we sell the right of somebody to take delivery of shares from us or to demand something from us in the trade, we have opened ourselves up to considerable risk. On the other hand, if we buy right then we are limited with our risk. That alone is a significant lesson. All option trades, no matter how sophisticated they are, depend on these two levers: the lever of increasing our risk and the lever of reducing our risk. Increasing our risk means we have given somebody control over what they can demand from us. Reducing our risk means we have bought the right to take delivery or demand something of the other options trader. Now, with reduced risk there often comes reduced profit. The most important aspect of this particular section is where I identify which of the option spread trades should be avoided and which ones to embrace and use. Surprisingly, many of the trades that are more sophisticated do not necessarily increase our profit potential. This is why I have identified the short and simple spread trades that give us unlimited profit potential with limited risk.

There are a lot of different strategies I have explained in this section. I mentioned which ones I prefer and which ones I think should be avoided. More important than having a large number of option trade strategies to talk about or potentially use is knowing which of a limited number of option strategies is needed in particular trading circumstances.

One of the aspects of virtually all option trading strategies is that we have to be neutral about the market, we have to see a bullish side to the market, or we have to see a bearish side to the market. In order to make the decision of bullish, bearish, or neutral, we have to have some means of assessing what the market is doing.

Once we understand all of these strategies, as explained in this chapter, as a set of tools that we can potentially use for different market trading conditions, the question becomes what those market conditions are at any one time. The next section will dive into assessing what the market is doing based on what are called technical indicators. The reason I am focusing on technical indicators and not fundamental analysis of underlying securities and options is that fundamental analysis does not play as large a role in short-term option trading.

5. Reading Tea Leaves - The Art of Practical Technical Analysis

For those not familiar with the terms fundamental analysis and technical analysis, they refer to different ways of assessing securities and the markets. Fundamental analysis refers to understanding the details of a particular company or market with reference to their profit and loss, the essentials of their specific customer base, and how they handle themselves on a business basis. A fundamental analysis will involve things like looking at the balance sheet of a company, looking at the income statement of the company analyzing the market share, and analyzing sales and product development. Fundamental analysis is not going to be the focus of most option traders who deal with short-term trades.

Technical analysis, on the other hand, deals with the variables expressed by the specific market, such as price, volume, open interest, moving averages of the price, relationships between different markets, relationships between securities and indexes, and a variety of other mathematical and graphical tools for understanding what is going on in a particular market.

Entire one-thousand-page volumes have been written about both fundamental analysis and technical analysis. All I will do is touch on some of the most basic tools I have used that I consider to be important for making decisions about how to trade options.

This is the section on technical analysis for determining whether we are going to approach our trades on a bullish stance, a bearish stance, or a neutral stance. Almost no aspect of financial trading or investing generates more controversy than technical analysis. There are plenty of people who will claim that technical analysis is entirely useless. Others will claim that while not useless, it is difficult to know who to believe when it comes to technical analysis even of the same charts for the same market conditions.

My experience has been definitive in terms of technical analysis. I have seen how some of the sharper technical analysts knew that the NASDAQ bubble was bursting and got themselves and their followers out well ahead of time. I also saw how technical analysis helped me determine when to enter the commodities market on the long side and when to enter on the short side with great regularity and great trading results. For the longer-term trend measured in five to twenty year segments, fundamental analysis will usually do better than technical analysis. For the short-term trend, however, technical analysis, in my opinion, will trump fundamental analysis almost every time.

There is so much to learn about technical analysis that all I can hope to do is introduce some of the basic concepts to give the reader a straightforward foundation for choosing broad potential moves within their trading focus.

Within technical analysis there are many varieties of schools, signals, and methods. For example, there is the very famous Elliott wave school analysis, the Dow theory schools, the volume schools, the turtle traders or the trend follower school, the swing trader school, and the reversal school. All of these different types of trading and analytical tools have their own systems they rely on whose adherents will very often swear by.

The tools I explain here are more general in nature and applicable across virtually any type of trading. They do not require years and years of study to master. They are simple to use, quick to execute, and relatively definitive in terms of their direction.

Basics of Trend Analysis: Macro, Micro, Mini:

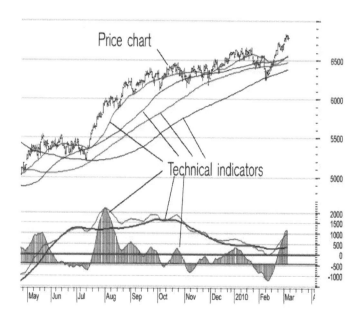

Source: Credit Suisse, A technical analysis chart.

First we have to understand what a trend is. Just as you would expect, a trend is the general direction the price or volume or whatever it is we are tracking is going in. If the price of Google was $800 on January 1 of 2013 and then moved up to $887, as it is today in October 2013, the trend for Google is up, or bullish.

Macro trends are much longer-term trends, generally from 1 1/2 years to 5 years or even longer.

Micro trends are going to be from a few months out to perhaps as long as a year and a half.

Mini-trends are what we are focus on. Mini-trends occur over a very short period of days, weeks, or months, at the most. Some day traders look at minutes. I will not cover that style of trading.

Both macro and micro trends are of very little use to this form of options trading. Mini-trends are trends that occur over very brief periods of time and are what will make or break us in our option trading strategies.

There are literally thousands of varieties of charts we can use to analyze the various options and their underlying securities, but I am going to recommend only two types of charts. You want to use a bar chart and a line chart. The type of bar chart you want is going to have an open price, a high price, a low price, and a close price.

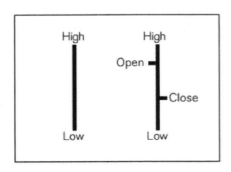

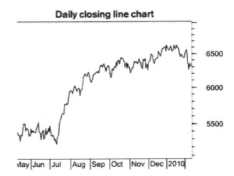

Daily closing line chart

Source: Credit Suisse. Examples of a bar chart and a line chart.

A line chart simply plots the price or volume of whatever we are analyzing over time using a line. Clear enough.

You can get lost in all kinds of candlestick charts and point-and-figure charts and similar kinds of variations, and they can certainly be useful for certain types of trading, but more often than not, the same knowledge can be gleaned by using the very simple bar chart and the line chart.

Chart Analysis

When looking at charts we are looking for concepts called resistance, support, moving averages, trend lines, and trend channels.

All of these are defined by the pictures shown below. Resistance is the point where a price or volume figure has attempted to surpass a level and has bounced back. Support is where something has bounced down to that level and reversed or returned up. Moving averages are calculated on a variety of different methods where we are looking for the overall average of a long-term series of prices or perhaps volumes.

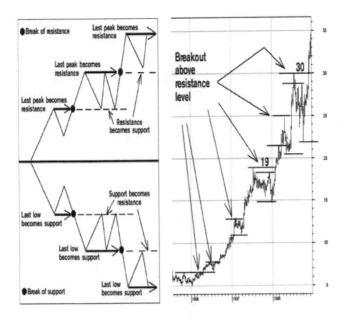

Source: Credit Suisse. Showing support and resistance lines.

A trend line is drawn from one lower or higher point of a line along the time axis to another higher or lower point of the line. It is a straight line between at least three points. When that trend line is broken, this often defines a new trend in the opposite direction.

A trend channel defines the high and low points of a price or volume line as it moves up or down in a particular trend. A break outside of the trend channel can often signify a change in the trend.

One of the important aspects of trends relates back to macro-, mini-, and micro-trends. Trading in the

82

direction of all of those trends agreeing will give us the highest probability of a positive trade. If we are in a situation where the mini-trend, which is the trend for a few days out to a few weeks, is trading opposite either the macro- or the micro-trends, then we had better have all of our technical ducks in a row to make sure we know exactly how long that mini-trend is going to last.

Technical Indicators

Some of the technical indicators used to analyze price and sometimes volume include moving average, momentum indicators, and relative strength indicators. I rarely use relative strength unless I am trading across markets.

Moving averages can be calculated for periods as short as three to five days or for longer periods of fifty-five days to forty or fifty-two weeks. Almost any variety of moving averages will give a line along the price line that shows the trend of the current price relative to that moving average.

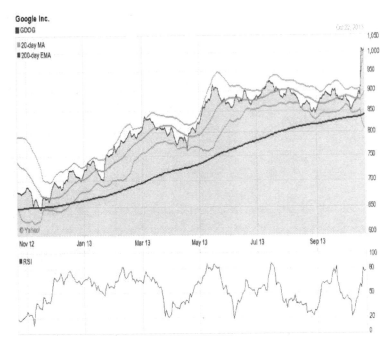

Source: Yahoo! Finance. Chart showing GOOG price with 20 moving average (20 DMA), 200 DMA, gray lines showing Bollinger bands—a trading channel—and the RSI reading below.

Momentum indicators relate to the speed of a change in price. They indicate whether a trend is accelerating or decelerating rather than what the actual price level is. Moving averages, as explained before, are lagging indicators after the price trend has already turned. Momentum indicators lead the price trend. They give a signal before the price trend begins to move in that direction. Momentum and moving average indicators work together. A momentum indicator will suggest that

84

a trend change is occurring, but the moving average indicator has to confirm that trend change in order to be verified.

I only use momentum indicators when the moving average (MA) indicators for the short term and longer term, say five-day MA and fifty-day MA, are in conflict. This guide focuses on the more certain trade where both short- and longer-term MA indicators agree. There is no reason to complicate trades by getting into more challenging technical situations.

Relative strength indicators are used to determine how a particular sector or security is performing in terms of momentum comparing recent gains to recent losses. RSI can help indicate overbought or oversold conditions. One of the reasons it can be an important indicator is that it helps us identify the strong and weak performers in a certain segment.

Defining Trends

The main task any trader faces, shorter-term options traders especially, is identifying the general trend of the security and the market they are trading. Fortunately, identifying trends is extremely easy to do. A trend line is defined by three points connected together along the price of the underlying security or market you are trading. A trend line shows whether a market is heading higher or lower for the time period covered by the trend line.

A trend line showing the bullish or upward price of EMC Corp over approximately 3 1/2 years.

Trend lines are easy to draw for strong up or down trends. When a market or security is bouncing around in price but not climbing or falling over the period, trends are much harder to discern. That is called a non-trending or neutral market. Many of the trades explained in this guide are for just such non-trending markets.

Even more useful than trend lines are trend channels. These are similar to trend lines, but with a top and bottom channel for clearly defining the top and bottom of price movements along the support and resistance levels.

Source: Stockcharts.com - A bearish, or downward, trend channel with the main trend shown in blue and the channel support level shown in red.

Though using trend lines and trend channels may appear to be old school and not competitive with high-speed trading software, it still allows traders to spot longer-term trends and reversals just as they always have. A good example of using trends and channels to spot a new bull market occurred in the recent multi-year increase in the S&P 500. A host of analysts spotted the potential for the S&P 500 to begin breaking out from a neutral or bearish trend.

Spotting Reversals

Spotting reversals involves checking the price action compared to several indicators. The first flashing signal for a reversal will be exactly as the chart above shows. The price will go either above or below the 20 DMA line or shorter-term MA. This is an early indicator of at least a short-term trend change. Short-term trend changes are often long enough for option trades expiring in a month or two.

The full confirmation of a trend change generally occurs when the price action crosses the 200 DMA.

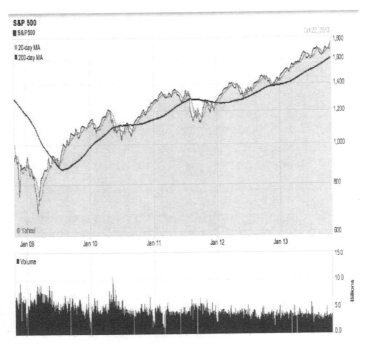

Source: Yahoo! Finance.
The green line shows the 20 DMA. It revealed the trend reversal months before it was confirmed by the 200 DMA. The new bullish trend was confirmed and has been running for four years. Notice how the 20

DMA can fake a trader out to either the up or down side, but the 200 DMA rarely sends a fake signal.

Different analysts use different timeframes for deciding when a reversal or trend change is confirmed, but the 200 DMA has been fairly reliable. As the example above shows, when the S&P 500 crossed the 200 DMA, it marked a definite trend reversal from a bearish and neutral market to a bullish market.

Spotting reversals can be one of the best forms of options trading, but it is a challenging task to get right the 52% of the time required for straight calls or puts. Using option spreads will push the odds dramatically in your favor because no longer are you confined to the long or short side of trading. You can make money just as easily, and often with less risk, by trading neutral, non-trending markets, without having to spot potential reversals.

Tops and Bottoms

Tops and bottoms mark the price points where a trend reversal takes place. They are notoriously challenging for most traders to spot. The temptation for spotting tops and bottoms for price is where that funny market saying "Bulls make money and bears make money, but pigs get slaughtered" comes from. The pig is the person who craves that last dollar in the transaction and wants to pick the exact top or bottom for their trade. While the tools I provide here will help greatly in that quest, it is a difficult task at best. More importantly, it is rarely if ever necessary to accurately predict the top and bottom of a trend or security price to make profitable trades.

Picking a top requires monitoring the price and volume action of the security. For example, the chart below shows both price and volume for GOOG.

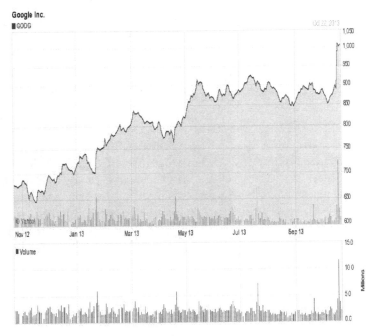

Source: Yahoo! Finance.
The volume spike demonstrates perfectly that securities of all kinds generally rise on high volume and fall on lower volume. Volume is shown in the bar chart below the price chart.

When volume is rising, price will tend to rise. If volume peaks and price continues to rise, that strongly suggests that there is a reversal to the downside dead ahead. Exactly this happened with GOOG, as shown by the above chart.

Spotting a bottom in any market is the reverse of spotting a top, with a few wrinkles thrown in.

If a securities price has been dropping while the volume is picking up, this strongly suggests that there will be a reversal to the upside shortly. Looking at the GOOG chart above, it also shows that there are rarely volume spikes to the downside. Just after a major price drop, there can be volume spikes as bargain hunters sweep in and begin bidding up the stock. That stampede marks a reversal.

Additional signals for determining tops and bottoms include a simple method of checking for repeated attempts at breaking either support or resistance. If a security attempts to break through previous resistance and fails on the third attempt, there is a strong chance that the price will head down hard immediately after the third attempt. The same tendency applies to bouncing through support levels.

Here is the support and resistance chart showing this pattern:

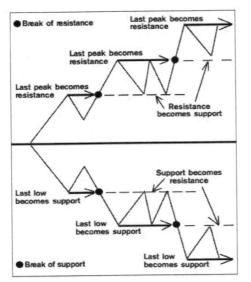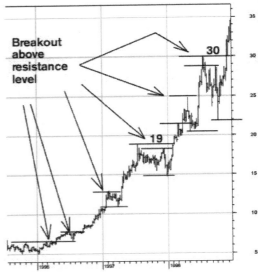

Source: Credit Suisse

The break of resistance shows a continuation of a bullish trend. If instead of breaking resistance the price backs off from the resistance line, a top is often reached. The same applies to price bouncing off support three times for defining a bottom. If a securities price bounces off support three times, it has probably bottomed for the time period and is heading higher in a new trend pattern.

As dirt simple as the three-touch rule sounds, you will be amazed at how reliable and repeatable this technical indicator is.

Non-Trending Markets

Prior to learning about option spread trading, non-trending markets could decimate an options trader. Once you learn about how to handle non-trending markets, you may find yourself hunting for nothing but non-trending markets.

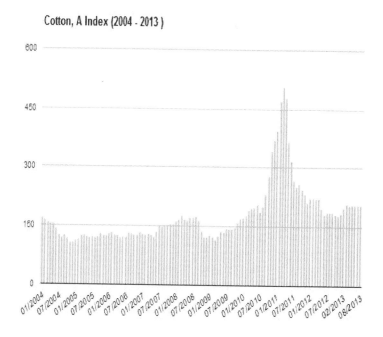

Cotton, A Index (2004 - 2013)

Source: Mongabay.
Cotton prices from 2004-2013 show a neutral, non-trending market from roughly 2004-2007. A trader going long had as much chance as a trader going short. But a trader using option spreads would have had a high probability of profitable trades as the neutral market would rarely bring out of the money options into the money.

As mentioned in the section on establishing trend lines and trend channels, a non-trending market can be called a neutral market, where there is not a definite trend either up or down, bullish or bearish. This means that straight calls and puts will often expire worthless, with traders losing the premiums paid and the commissions. Not the way to build a fortune!

These kinds of markets are characterized by lower volume and limited price movements that last a short time in either direction. A trend line will show that there is little if any angle of ascent for defining a bull market or descent for defining a bear market.

The cotton chart below shows a perfect example of a non-trending market from 2004-2007. The best way to profit in a directionless market is one of the main topics of this options spread trading guide. Virtually any of the option spreads for neutral markets could have yielded well above-average profit probabilities. A trend line would have been flat or horizontal, showing that neutral strategies were the way to benefit.

Trend Following

Trend following means choosing trades in the direction of the trend lines. This is the surest way to stack the odds of profit in our favor. When the trend lines are pointed upwards for defining a bullish trend, we want to pursue bullish-oriented trades. When the trend lines are pointed downwards for a bearish trend, our trades should be oriented to profit from going short primarily.

As simple as this seems, there will be a temptation to call trend reversals tops or bottoms. Fight that temptation. The trades I discuss in this guide are designed for trend following for the most part. There is a good reason for sticking with the trend instead of trading against it. When a trader places trades that require the prices to move against the major trend, there is a shorter timeframe for the trade to be profitable. An example of this type of mistake would be trading on the bearish side of the metals market from 2001-2006. Though there were many dips, the general direction was bullish. In order to trade profitably against the bullish trend, a trader not only had to pick the right entry point, but also had to pick the right exit point. For the silver market, the entry and exit points often had to be exact to the day and even hour for a counter-trend trader to make a profit. Though it is possible for an experienced trader to make those kinds of trades, it creates a significant burden for choosing the times and price points more accurately than most of us are capable of doing.

I will trade against the trend on two conditions:

1) If there is a parabolic rise in the price of a security. Parabolic rises *always* end in a severe drop after the peak of the rise. This is one of the rare absolutes in trading. This point alone is probably worth your full investment for this guide. Whenever you see a parabolic rise, back up the truck and load up options on the short side, because when the price peaks, it will fall hard almost instantly. This happened with the NASDAQ, with gold in 1980, and it just happened with GOOG, as shown above!

2) When news hits a stock or security unreasonably hard. This will tend to crush a stock for a very brief period of time, but it will almost immediately bounce

back. I rarely trade based on this criterion, though it is fairly reliable.

Trading with the trend makes picking the entry and exit points far less important because time becomes our ally. If we choose to run against the established trend, we have a limited time to wring the profit out of our trade. While it is certainly possible to get our time envelope close, we are making more work for ourselves than we need to. Choose to follow the trends and the price action can often rescue you from sometimes incorrect entry points. When we are trading opposite the trend, we are not going to get rescued. We are going to get barbecued by the major trend.

Basic Tools for Analysis

Today's traders have almost too many tools at their disposal. I use Yahoo! Finance charts, as you can see from the several I used already. They are simple to set up, have reasonable market delays, and allow for the key technical indicators. My options trading brokerage, OptionsXpress, offers technical tools much like those of other brokerage houses. Using your brokerage tools has the advantage of allowing you to set limits on charts for warnings, entry and exit points, watch alerts for when options enter the zones you may set up, and other useful tools.

The main resources an options trader needs are:

- Options pricing calculator. This helps for planning trades, determining intrinsic value, premiums, and time decay, etc.

- Trend lines for 20 DMA, 200 DMA, volume, Bollinger bands, RSI, and any other indicators you feel comfortable with. More indicators does not necessarily make for better trading performance. The key is matching the indicators to the type of trading you are doing, exactly as described here. All a trader needs for successful spread trading is to determine the major trend, or lack of it, plus potential tops and bottoms for counter-trend moves, if desired.

- Options monitoring up-to-date pricing, order fills, and status.

- Possibly an options analysis package like OptionsVue or Options Smart. Though these tools can be useful, the best way to start option spread trading is to stick with the basics. Many traders, especially in an area as fast-paced as options trading, have a tendency to look for tool after tool for creating the perfect trading system. While many have claimed just such a system, the top traders, such as Trader Vic Sperandeo, one of the finest traders who has traded profitably for decades, use simple tools like those explained here. I know because I learned almost everything I know about trading from Trader Vic!

With these basic but useful technical analysis tools in your tool belt, you are ready to wade into the waters of options spread trading. Each step of the way, I will explain the reasoning for how to choose the sector to trade, the vehicle to trade, the months to trade, price points, and the type of options spread.

At first these choices will seem foreign and difficult to follow. That feeling will pass quickly as you see the patterns emerging for how one decision follows naturally from the technical analysis foundation to the easy principles of choosing an option spread strategy based on risk tolerance and market perspective.

Soon enough, the decisions will seem easy to you. You will have a few favorite options spread trades that you prefer for each type of market you will run into. This is when the fun and profit really begins. When you arrive at the point where you can easily assess the type of option for the market conditions, you will be well on your way to having a high probability of having profitable trades. You will be an advanced options trader.

Being an advanced options trader will turn formerly mundane markets into more interesting ones. I recall that when I first started trading options in college, all I knew how to do was go long or go short. I would buy call options when I thought a stock may rise and buy put options when I thought a stock may fall. I had some hits and a lot of misses.

I read all of the books about the Black-Scholes pricing model. Despite having a good math background from engineering, I did not see the relationship to what I was experiencing in the market. While famous for creating the options pricing model, Black and Scholes are not famous like Trader Vic for becoming rich from trading options! They made a lot of money creating models for others who made a lot more money. The main lesson I learned was not to overcomplicate my trading and to learn about the wide variety of trades for all types of markets. That is exactly what this guide will bring you: simple techniques explained thoroughly for a beginning options spread trader to take and run with, at a much higher level of success than trading the basic long or short side of any market.

Stock/Commodity Selection

Having some technical tools to work with is the first step to entering the options marketplace. One of the burdens for all traders is choosing the market they would like to trade. The options trading market is somewhat easier to navigate than the general investing market because options are more restricted then stocks, commodities, mutual funds, and ETFs (exchange traded funds).

The reason the options marketplace is more restricted than perhaps stocks or commodities or other types of investments, is because not all investments allow options. There are a large number of stocks and funds, as well as commodities where options are either limited or not available at all.

I have given an example from when I was trading copper and how I wanted to find options on copper futures but there were none trading within the range I needed or the ones that were trading did not have sufficient volume for me to enter and exit the trade easily. This is not uncommon in a lot of commodity markets. This is also something that happens with thinly traded stocks and thinly traded exchange funds. So keep in mind when you decide to enter into a certain sector whether there is enough trading volume and interest for you to find options that meet the trade criteria you require for sending the probabilities for profit in your favor.

Some of the best areas to look for stock options include index options, large stock options such as Google and General Electric and all of the Dow components, all of the leading NASDAQ components, etc. Taking options in the commodities market becomes much more challenging because there are a large number of futures trading in the commodity sector and few options available for them or because the options market is extremely thinly traded.

Beginner option traders and those new to trading spreads are recommended to trade either index options or large capitalization stock options. Steer clear for your initial learning period of the commodities market. Navigating the commodities futures market for finding the right options to trade at the right time at the right strike price will be quite a hassle in several of the commodities markets. The two markets I consider exceptions to this rule, and ones that I have traded in extensively, are the gold and silver markets.

The majority of option traders are engaged in the stock market generally, so I will focus most examples on the stock market and only pepper in a few examples from the commodities market.

Choosing the Sector First

Choosing the sector first means deciding which sector of the market you are going to trade in a particular direction. Taking 2013 as an example, the year started off positively with an upward trend from the beginning of January. However, this was not the case across all sectors of the market. Materials producers and commodity-oriented companies saw that their stock prices either went down or went virtually nowhere for most of the year. So choosing the correct sector, such as healthcare or financial stocks for 2013, would have a dramatic impact on the direction of the trend you were going to trade.

If you have decided that you want to trade indexes, this applies to you, too. There are a number of different indexes to choose from, including the Dow Jones industrial average, the S&P 500, and the NASDAQ. For those old enough to remember trading during the dot-com bubble, the Dow Jones industrial average was doing virtually nothing during the same period that the NASDAQ was skyrocketing and crashing.

For 2013, the S&P 500 and the Dow Jones industrial average were both tracking positively. This means that you could trade either of these indexes and have a similar trend. However, if you decided that you wanted to trade the HUI index for miners, the trend would be completely different—to the downside. I mention all of this so that you understand that choosing a sector sets you up for identifying a much clearer trend to follow. Choosing an index can often mean choosing large-cap stocks, small-cap stocks, technology stocks, or any other variety of stocks you want to focus on. The same rules apply with an index that largely applies to an individual stock or a commodities market.

Let's say that I have decided I want to trade options on the Dow. The Dow Jones industrial average is composed of thirty of the largest industrial stocks trading on the big board for the most part. The Dow was up roughly 19% for 2013 as of this writing. This establishes a firm upward trend or bullish trend for the Dow Jones industrial average.

By selecting my sector, in this case large-cap stocks with the Dow industrial average, I was easily able to determine what the trend was for my sector.

I have not drawn any trend lines, but the 19% increase since the beginning of the year establishes little doubt that I am dealing with positive sloping trend lines.

Choose Direction

You might think that seeing a positive sloping trend line and a clear bullish bias to the progress of the Dow is the same as choosing direction. It is close, but not quite the same. The reason that choosing direction is different from choosing the sector and the trend line is that I could quite easily decide to trade counter trend. I have often traded counter trend in the metals markets. I tend not to trade counter trend in the stock markets and suggest the same for most traders. The reason for this is that the metals market has developed an almost predictable pattern of getting squashed as option expiration time comes near. It was easy to trade the counter trend with those moves. The stock market does not often have these repeatable trends. The reason for this is that stock market capitalization is much larger than the tiny metals markets that I was trading.

As I recommend for most traders, beginning or advanced, I will follow my own advice and trade with the trend. The direction I am choosing is long-side or bullish-oriented spreads based on the positive trend shown from the 19% increase of the Dow since the beginning of the year.

Choosing to trade with the trend now gives me more flexibility and adds a higher degree of probability for successful trading. The key benefit of trading with the trend is that my entry and exit points will be more forgiving, and it also tilts my strategies in a clearer direction. The trader who decides to potentially go counter trend is going to have to make a decision between going bullish, going neutral, and going bearish. Choosing between the bullish or long-oriented option spreads and the neutral-oriented option spreads or the bearish or short-side option spread opens up a virtually unlimited number of choices for a trader. Having too many choices is not a good thing. When I trade with the trend, I only have a limited number of trades I can use successfully. As opposed to the three types of directional trades, I am now limited to at most two of the trades. The two trades I would potentially use in a market such as the bullish Dow Jones trade are either neutral or bullish, with a heavy tilt in favor of the bullish side. I have already eliminated two thirds or more of potential option strategies and taken the probabilities of a successful trade to almost 33% higher relative to engaging in counter-trend trading. Though this reasoning seems incredibly simpleminded and basic, and a reader may think that everybody would do exactly that kind of thing because it is so obvious, I can assure you that many traders go counter trend, attempt to pick the top or bottom, or use neutral strategies when the market is clearly operating with a bullish or bearish bias.

Our simple determination of a strong upward bullish trend eliminates most of our potential option strategies. That is exactly what I want. I do not want to have every strategy as a potential for the market, with each one representing a small chance of a successful trade. I want my reading of the market to indicate a narrow band of potentially successful trades that have a much higher probability of earning a profit, or at least of not losing my investment capital.

Choose Timeframe

An entire book could be written on choosing the correct timeframe for options trades. The majority of option spread trades will use time decay to the advantage of the trade. For this reason, the time horizons that option spread trades tend to focus on are much narrower than either long-side or short-side-only option trades. Many of my copper option trades and metal markets option trades had durations of months before options expiration. I traded that way because I knew the seasonal variations and was not always spread trading. I was taking long or short positions. I was not using time decay to my advantage. Time decay generally worked against my trades. The reason I chose long- or short-side-only trades in some of these markets was because I had very clear readings on the direction of the market over the time I was trading. I was essentially opting for only long or short positions because of my high confidence in my market analysis.

The type of trading you will be doing with this guide will be much shorter in duration. Many of the trades will only allow for near-term month expiration, or the month after the near-term month.

Deciding Which Horse to Ride, Specific Vehicle for your Options Trade

Once you have decided the general market and perhaps the specific sector you want to trade, you must choose the specific vehicle or security for your options trade. This line of reasoning assumes you are not going to engage in cross-market spreads, inter-commodity spreads, or inter-sector spreads. All you want to do in choosing a specific vehicle is make sure that there is the kind of action you need in order to get in and out of your option trade with a minimum of slippage. Slippage is when you place an order to buy or sell at a certain target and the order cannot be filled at that specific target because the market is not sufficient in terms of volume to fill the order. Slippage can also occur if you happen to have a broker that doesn't have an efficient order processing system. Most brokers will promise nearly instant fills if there is an available market.

When I engage in an options trade, one of the first things I look at is the volume of trades on that option. Let's take a look at Google's options:

945.00	GOOG131116P00945000	58.67	↑1.63	60.50	63.20	1	32
945.00	GOOG7131116P00945000	61.10	↓8.20	60.40	63.20	75	7
950.00	GOOG7131101P00950000	65.60	0.00	63.30	66.40	26	10
950.00	GOOG131116P00950000	60.43	↓23.47	64.80	67.20	11	20
950.00	GOOG7131116P00950000	73.30	0.00	64.80	68.00	1	19
955.00	GOOG7131101P00955000	80.00	0.00	67.90	71.00	10	10
955.00	GOOG131116P00955000	79.79	0.00	69.60	71.90	12	23
955.00	GOOG7131116P00955000	98.30	0.00	69.30	72.20	6	6
960.00	GOOG131116P00960000	75.25	↑6.18	73.60	76.50	20	32
965.00	GOOG131116P00965000	79.75	↓1.64	77.70	81.00	20	10
970.00	GOOG131116P00970000	77.97	0.00	82.50	85.60	21	32

The put options above show a variety of strike prices for a November put on Google. Notice how the strike price at $945 has seventy-five in the volume column with an open interest of seven. Moving down to the strike price of $950, there is a volume of one with an open interest of nineteen.

The lesson here is not to trade the options with very low volume and to go straight to the options with higher volume. There is the possibility that you will be doing what is known as crowding an options trade. You are not jumping on this option strictly because there is sufficient volume for you to trade and it is a popular option to buy or sell. Rather, you are choosing to buy or sell an option that meets all of your criteria, including the volume and open-interest criteria. As discussed in the previous chapter, part of the criteria involves determining whether you are trading with or against the trend. If there happens to be an option that has significant volume and open interest and yet is going against your trading plan and trend, that is not the option to choose.

In the case of a November put for Google, there are several strike prices that have sufficient volume for most option trades that a beginner would engage in. There are only two strike prices that are clearly insufficiently traded for a beginner to get involved with. The $945 strike price and the $950 strike price should be left alone. You will notice that there are multiple $950 strike prices and multiple $945 strike prices. These strike prices are listed on Yahoo! Finance but may not be listed by most brokers because they are adjusted option prices. They can be ignored. Most brokerages are going to show strictly one option at one strike price at a certain expiration date and will not cloud the trader screen with multiple options that may not directly translate to the one hundred shares of stock as the option should.

To summarize, choose a sufficient volume and open interest for the sector and option you want to trade. This is another area that seems extremely obvious, and yet you can tell that there are option traders on Google options right now who are more or less stuck taking whatever the dealer can find for them when they decide they want to get out of their option trade. The reason for this is that they didn't follow the simple rule of only entering option trades in sectors where there is sufficient volume to buy or sell virtually instantly.

Select the Type of Trade

Determining what level of bullishness, bearishness, or neutrality you want to take on in the trade is also important. For a simple 100% bull trade, I could just buy a call option. This assumes that I have determined that the trend is up or bullish for the sector and the specific vehicle I'm choosing to trade. The same applies for a put option, that is, a 100% bullish or 100% bearish position. It's also not the smartest way to approach trades. The reason for option spread trading is avoiding the strictly defined bullish or bearish side almost entirely.

Recalling the huge number of trades possible that were explained in the Chapter 3, the methods for choosing the type of trade to get involved with is simply picking from the bullish, bearish, or neutral trades defined below.

Neutral strategies are as follows:

- ratio spread
- calendar straddle
- the condor
- the straddle
- the iron butterfly
- the iron condor
- the strangle

Bullish strategies include:

- covered straddle
- bull calendar spread
- call back spread
- bull call spread
- the collar
- covered calls
- naked puts
- bearish strategies include:

- naked calls
- covered puts
- bear put spread
- put back spread

These strategies comprise part of the selection choice for determining the type of trade to enter based on the trend line direction as defined from the technical analysis section. After you determine the trend of the sector you wish to trade, it should be noted that sometimes you go back and forth in terms of deciding whether you want to find a sector that is in a bullish or bearish direction, for example. Then you look for a vehicle for the trade.

Of all the strategies defined under each of the categories, there are clearly superior ones that should be used more often than not. I clarified which ones to avoid when I described all the varieties of trades that were available. Some of them simply make no sense to enter into from our risk reduction perspective.

The most complicated area to choose a strategy in is generally neutral markets. There are so many neutral strategies, referring to the situation when a trader doesn't know whether the market is headed up or down or would simply rather trade for low volatility, that it becomes more of a challenge to figure out which strategies to choose than in either the bullish or the bearish categories.

A few of the preferred neutral spread trades to use include:

- neutral calendar spread
- butterfly spread and variations

- condor and variations

The bullish spread trades I recommend also include some trades that others may consider to be neutral-oriented trades. The reason I recommend them as bullish trades as well is that they are oriented toward greater profit if the trend continues to be bullish, though they will also profit if there is low volatility prior to the options expiring.

My recommended bullish-oriented option spread trades include:

- bull calendar spread
- bull call spread
- bull put spread
- diagonal bull call
- call back spread

There are many other bullish strategies, with names like married put and uncovered put write, but they do not offer significant advantages over the ones I have chosen and introduce significant complications.

The recommended bearish-oriented option spread trades will be essentially the same as the bullish ones but in reverse:

- put back spread
- diagonal bear put spread
- bear call spread
- bear put spread

Though there are many other bearish and bullish option spread strategies, the ones above limit the risk and present reasonable profit opportunities.

110

Plan for Riding the Trade

One of the great traders, who formed the basis of the famous movie *Trading Places* with Eddie Murphy and Dan Akroyd, was Richard Dennis. The school of trading he founded is known as "Turtle Traders." It is essentially a strictly technical form of trading, with trend following regarded as the key element to success. Dennis had years of successful trading behind him when he recruited complete novices to train in his methodology. He instructed them that it almost did not matter how you entered a trade, but that what was important was how you rode the trade from your entry point.

I consider that to be an extreme statement with a kernel of truth to it. I experienced this effect multiple times in my own career when I advised others on how to trade options. To my complete shock, I found that giving someone advice about what to buy and when was only half the battle. If I did not watch their trade for them, they would find ways to miss the best profit opportunity. I watched as I recommended bearish spreads on a few industrial metals using stocks as proxies. The copper market would fall as I had predicted, and the stocks were along for the ride, but the people I was advising would not know when to hold for more profit, sell immediately, or cut losses short, if that happened to be the case.

While we can set automatic stops, some trades have too much volatility, where the option prices bounce up and down too much to set a 10% or 20% stop that automatically sells out our position. These trades need our eyeballs and our own plan for when the technical conditions are met for closing out our position. Fortunately, spread trading can minimize the downside of our trade, making watching each trade slightly less critical than straight bullish or bearish positions. But our profits are based just as much on how we enter a trade as how we exit it.

Before I enter a trade, I create a trading plan. My plan includes the following:

- Sector: small-cap, large-cap, tech, financials, consumer staples, commodities, metals, etc.

- Sector major trend: bullish, bearish, non-trending/neutral

- Underlying security: the stock, index, commodity, or instrument the option is based on.

- Option(s) traded: calls and puts with strike prices and expiration with 1-4 options.

- Strategies applied: one or more of the option strategies explained in Chapter 3.

- Expected trade duration: date I expect to close the trade, or expiration.

Max Loss Allowed: Based on account position and personal limits for losses. I recommend never allowing a loss of more than 5% of your trading capital on any one trade. That translates to the guideline that for every $10k in your account, you want to limit a trading loss to $500 per trade if at all possible. Even better is if you can risk the recommended 2% or less on any one trade. This recommendation was clarified by Larry Hite in Jack Schwager's *Market Wizards,* published in 1989. Hite originally stated that a trader should risk only 1% on any trade. That would be ideal, but it is also hard to manage for traders just starting out. The top end for trading is 5%. As much as I hate to admit it, when I started trading at the age of twelve (through my father's broker), I risked it all. I continued this foolish level of risky trading until I gained a significant portfolio. If you can keep your risk to under 2%, great. The odds are that you may have to risk a higher percentage initially until you develop enough of an account to reach the recommended risk level. More on this in the risk management section.

Triggers for Quick Close: What events would change my anticipated profit scenario into a high-probability loss scenario? This relates to a trend change, a reversal, a financial shock such as when Lehman Brothers went under, etc. If one of these triggers pops up, I close my trade immediately, irrespective of the loss or profit.

Potential Upside: Maximum potential profit, or unlimited upside.

Potential Downside: This will usually be limited and defined by the option spread strategies I focus on. Occasionally I engage in selling call or put options that could open me to unlimited losses.

Probability of Profit: This comes from using options calculators and running some scenarios through databases of probabilities for various markets and stocks.

Options calculator:
http://www.optionsprofitcalculator.com/

Theoretical pricing options calculators:
http://www.volatilitytrading.net/optioncalculator.htm

These calculators will help us identify our risk levels, potential profit, and general probability for profit with a particular options trade.

This is an average expectation for success and tells me if I am expecting a miracle where the potential for profit is 3% or something ridiculously low or if I am on the side with the right odds of over 60%. This is not a definite source of profitable trades, but it is a good indicator of how the trade may go.

I generally do not day trade. I trade when I have the odds stacked in my favor. There are always good trades available in almost all markets where there is enough volume. Using a trading set-up plan like the one I use, or one you develop, is the key to removing the emotions from trading. Knowing why I am in a trade, what my probabilities are, and why I would bounce out of the trade makes riding the trade a bit like following a working GPS to a destination. A trading plan is not nearly as definite in guiding us to profit, but it dramatically increases our chances of managing our trade to the desired profitable end, or at least minimizing potential losses.

6. Trade Setups - Putting On a Winning Spread Position

Trading has a lot in common with athletics. Both trading and athletics require focusing on and perfecting the basics. Both require mental toughness in dealing with conditions on the athletic field or the trading screen. More than anything, both require the ability to deal with occasional losses and continue working your system.

I happen to enjoy playing chess, though I cannot claim to be an extremely strong player yet, because it involves many of the same skills as trading. I have to analyze the chessboard and the market to find opportunities to advance my position. The market, or my chess challenger, is there to take my resources as quickly as possible. If I read the chessboard or the market correctly and plan how to advance in the market or on the board with the correct strategy, I increase my chances of winning dramatically. The great chess masters, and the great trading masters, all use a checklist prior to executing their moves. Without the checklist, they open themselves up to what is known on the chessboard as a "blunder." You and I call it a loss, or getting crushed by the market. Whatever it is called, we want to avoid the stupid blunders caused by ignoring the basics of sound trading practices.

Putting All the Tools Together

This section gives you a trading checklist for putting all of the potential strategies together. It is possible that you are already comfortable with the basics of analysis and selecting sectors and specific options to jump right into trading. I recommend holding off and going through a few of these trades with me. There are always gray areas in trading when it comes to reading the market, and some of the trades below will offer you insights into how to navigate when you are in the running river of a fast market.

As an example, I am going to jump into trading the Dow Jones industrial average index. I happen to like this index for trades because it is composed of thirty of the largest industrial-oriented companies and has some nice trend characteristics. Specifically, the Dow Jones industrial average index has lower volatility than trading commodity indexes, smaller capitalization stocks, and certainly less than individual commodities.

You can of course choose almost any security in virtually any market that offers options. The one qualification to that is that you are able to get enough data in the form of graphs, charts, and up-to-date quotes as well as volume for you to evaluate the technical details necessary for creating a trade.

With the DJIA, I have chart data going back about as far as the stock market goes back.

Analysis First

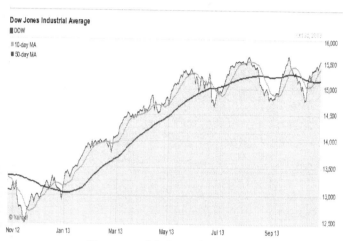

Source: Yahoo Finance

The chart above shows the Dow Jones industrial average for the past six months. I chose a six-month timeframe because I wanted this example to focus on an options trade expiring within thirty to sixty days at the outside. With that short timeframe in mind, I was able to focus on a six-month timeframe for the chart rather than a year, two years, or five years. It is quite possible to have a counter trend rally that can go on for as long as six months or more in a secular bear market. This is probably not the case here, as there has been a general uptrend for multiple years, so I will not analyze it on a counter-trend basis.

Depending on whether you are seeing the chart in color or not, the basic chart itself shows a steady movement from approximately 12,500 up to 15,500 over the past six months. The single line that is moving approximately along the peaks and valleys of the main Dow shaded chart is the ten-day moving average. The other line showing a steady movement along the general trend of the Dow chart, or red line, is the fifty-day moving average. It shows the ten-day moving average to determine whether the average was in danger of crossing through the major fifty-day trend. With the Dow Jones industrial average comfortably above the fifty-day and the ten-day moving averages and showing bullish movement over the entire chart as explained with the climb from 12,500 to 15,500, I have full confirmation that the major trend and the current minor trend are bullish.

I could possibly begin further analysis to determine whether there is a reversal point coming. The reason this is unnecessary is because of the agreement of the short- and longer-term trends with no reversal already beginning. As I recommended in earlier sections, calling reversals is a fairly challenging thing to do and gives away the main advantage of trend following and trend-direction trading.

I have established that the trend is bullish and that both short- and longer-term trend lines are confirming the overall movement of the index. This means I will select a bullish-oriented option spread trading strategy. I can also select a more neutral option spread trading strategy with a bullish tilt.

Choosing Directions

The analysis from the previous section makes it very clear that the direction of the DJIA is bullish or upward.

Though it might seem obvious that I would enter into a bullish trade based on the analysis of the major trend, I separate the analysis from choosing the direction of the trade because they are not the same thing. The analysis tells me what the major trend and the minor trend are for the graph's timeframe. Even if the trend is bearish generally, I could choose a direction for a bullish trade because I'm expecting a reversal.

Choosing a direction will generally follow your overall trading methodology. I strongly recommend trend following so that the analysis almost automatically determines taking the answer regarding trend direction and simply applying that to your trade. A good example of when to choose an opposite direction trade or a reversal trade is in both the gold and silver markets that I enjoy trading in. Both gold and silver have frequent and severe reversals that become relatively easy to call, even in strong bull and upward-trending markets. Each security in each type of market you trade has its own characteristics you can learn over time, or you can find somebody who is an expert on the seasonality and the linkages between the market in the security you wish to trade and other leading indicators.

Getting back to our trade of the Dow Jones industrial average index. My trade direction is going to be bullish-oriented with the possibility of using a neutral strategy with a bullish orientation. This rules out bearish-oriented strategies or neutral-oriented strategies with a bearish tilt.

Choosing the Option Spread Strategy

Going back to the list in Chapter 5, I select the bullish calendar spread as my strategy. I could have selected almost any of the bullish or even possibly the neutral option strategies. I am choosing the bull calendar because it is a relatively simple option spread strategy that gives us unlimited profit if the trend continues and a limited downside if the trend reverses.

A bull calendar spread meets our conditions nicely for DJIA. It has unlimited upside profit if the DJIA continues the trend, as it shows it will probably do over the next 30-60 days, and it has a limited downside risk. My downside risk will only be what I invested to get into the trade.

A bull calendar spread involves selling an OTM call that expires relatively soon and buying a longer-term OTM call.

My plan is that the OTM call I sell will expire worthless, while I get to ride the longer-term call for an unlimited profit to the upside.

Choosing Timeframes

I am choosing to sell a November OTM call and buy a December OTM call. The reason for choosing these months has to do with trading volumes and my analysis timeframe. A longer-term trade out to March or September expiration would require a longer timeframe for potential profit, and my analysis would not have been as reliable because I looked at only six months of trading and the trading volumes were significantly lower at the strike prices I wanted. For all of these reasons, I chose much earlier expiration months with sufficient volume for me to enter and exit trades easily.

Choosing Vehicles

Here is the relevant list for the options:

154.00	DJX131101C00154000	1.57	0.00	1.95	2.14	96	96
154.00	DJX131116C00154000	2.24	0.00	2.42	2.52	9	863
155.00	DJX131101C00155000	1.07	↑0.08	1.15	1.27	9	32
155.00	DJX131116C00155000	1.76	↑0.32	1.72	1.82	13	2,792
156.00	DJX131101C00156000	0.55	↑0.15	0.52	0.63	26	22
156.00	DJX131116C00156000	1.22	↑0.12	1.16	1.26	75	290
157.00	DJX131101C00157000	0.17	0.00	0.16	0.25	15	15
157.00	DJX131116C00157000	0.75	0.00	0.72	0.80	10	186
158.00	DJX131116C00158000	0.44	0.00	0.42	0.49	5	486
159.00	DJX131116C00159000	0.30	0.00	0.22	0.29	3	86
160.00	DJX131116C00160000	0.12	0.00	0.11	0.17	56	304
161.00	DJX131116C00161000	0.07	0.00	0.05	0.11	10	41
162.00	DJX131116C00162000	0.06	0.00	0.01	0.07	11	51
163.00	DJX131116C00163000	0.06	0.00	N/A	0.06	50	56

Source: Yahoo Finance

The chart above shows the DJX options list for November 13 expiration and strike prices between 154 and 163. This equates to 15,400 and 16,300 on the DJIA. DJIA currently trades at 15,590. Based on the patterns I identified on the chart, I am choosing to sell the 160 strike price call that expires on November 16, 2013. This gives me roughly two weeks of trading. While I could have cut things closer with a 157-159 strike price, the heavy bullish pattern I established during the analysis suggests that this would be asking for the calls to go ITM. I can run volatility and probability analysis on each price point, but 160 has the best combination of distance for the average to go before options expiry and a much higher premium for me to pocket than the 161 strike price.

I will buy a December call at the same strike price of
160. Here is the chart for that call:

154.00	DJX131221C00154000	2.14	0.00	3.35	3.50	2	41
155.00	DJX131221C00155000	2.84	↑0.25	2.77	2.86	85	1,685
156.00	DJX131221C00156000	2.11	↑0.30	2.22	2.31	20	276
157.00	DJX131221C00157000	1.80	↑0.21	1.75	1.82	30	141
158.00	DJX131221C00158000	1.23	0.00	1.34	1.40	3	42
159.00	DJX131221C00159000	0.97	0.00	1.00	1.06	20	21
160.00	DJX131221C00160000	0.70	0.00	0.72	0.79	3	3,061
162.00	DJX131221C00162000	0.18	0.00	0.36	0.42	1	1
165.00	DJX131221C00165000	0.10	0.00	0.11	0.17	30	415
168.00	DJX131221C00168000	0.09	0.00	0.03	0.09	2	17

Source: Yahoo Finance

Though the volume is low at 160, I am only entering
one order, and it has significant open interest. My net
debit to enter this trade is (0.70 - 0.12) = $0.58 x 100 =
$580.

Watching Options Mechanics to Avoid Friction Costs

A few things about actually buying and selling options.
Spread trades require more transactions than just a
call or a put. Condors and butterflies can rack up four
times the commission fees of one-sided options such
as calls or puts. Those fees add up fast.

There are a variety of pricing plans from different
brokers. OptionsXpress, OptionsHouse, and
TradeKing all have lower costs than the major full-

service firms, but you have to select one that meets your trading style. I use OptionsXpress because their flat rate works for my style of trading and investing. TradeKing is a good choice for someone just getting started.

Riding the Trade

My downside will be known within the expiration date of the OTM call I sold. It will decay to worthlessness by November 16 if all goes according to my charts.

My probabilities are as follows:

I used a simple Monte Carlo simulator to check risk and potential profitability from one of the options calculators.

I am using the calculator at http://www.optionstrategist.com/calculators/probability for a simple analysis. These are not completely "accurate," per se, but simple indicators for average probabilities of a trade.

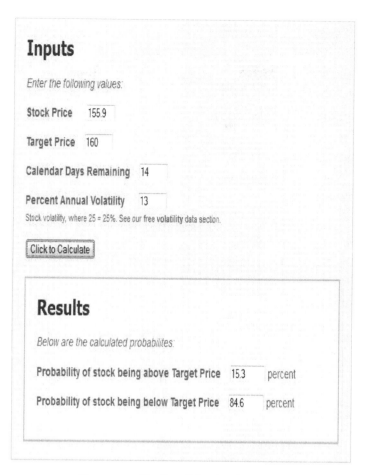

Inputs

Enter the following values:

Stock Price 155.9

Target Price 160

Calendar Days Remaining 14

Percent Annual Volatility 13

Stock volatility, where 25 = 25%. See our free volatility data section.

[Click to Calculate]

Results

Below are the calculated probabilites:

Probability of stock being above Target Price 15.3 percent

Probability of stock being below Target Price 84.6 percent

Source: OptionStrategist.com

I chose today's prices for the current stock price, then the strike price for the target. I used the VIX reading for today as the percentage volatility, though that method is debatable because the SP500 and DJX are heavily correlated.

The odds stack strongly in my favor for a profitable trade, with an 84.6% chance that the call I sold for November 16 will expire worthless.

Now for calculating the potential for profit.

Free Probability Calculator

Calculate stock market probabilities with this easy to use Monte Carlo simulation program. Get more results using McMillan's **Probability Calculator Software**.

Inputs

Enter the following values:

Stock Price 155.9

Target Price 160

Calendar Days Remaining 44

Percent Annual Volatility 13

Stock volatility, where 25 = 25%. See our free **volatility** data section.

[Click to Calculate]

Results

Below are the calculated probabilites:

Probability of stock being above Target Price 28.2 percent

Probability of stock being below Target Price 71.7 percent

Source: OptionStrategist.com

The farther out the simulation runs, the less reliable the results will be. Still, it gives a perspective that the likelihood of earning a profit is higher by 12.9% (28.2%-15.3%). That is more than enough of a difference to justify a trade.

One general note about options trading. The farther out you buy your option, the less the time decay of the option will affect you. As you may remember, time decay is the decrease in the value of the option based on getting closer to the expiration date of the option.

In this example, I used the very near-term time decay of the call I sold in my favor. The time decay for the December call is not quite as fast as the November call, with about a thirty-day difference, giving my call more of an opportunity to move into the money.

Here is how my trade plan looks for this bull calendar spread trade (note that you can use a spreadsheet for setting up your own trade plan; it does not need to be fancy and you do not need an automatic trading system):

Sector: Large-cap Index

Sector Major Trend: Bullish

Underlying Security: DJIA

Option(s) Traded: Sell Nov DJIA Call @160 ID DJX131116C00160000
                Buy Dec DJIA Call @160 ID DJX131221C00160000

Strategies Applied: Bull Calendar Spread

Expected Trade Duration: Between Nov Call going worthless and highest profit point reached before Dec Call expires based on trend analysis. Probably 25 day trade.

Max Loss Allowed: Amount of trade $580.00

Triggers for Quick Close: Not necessary as downside is limited.

Potential Upside: Unlimited based on the price of DJIA rising.

Potential Downside: Limited to cost of entering the trade at $580.00

Probability of Profit: 85% chance the call I sold expires worthless. 73% the call I bought goes ITM based on Monte Carlo simulation. The odds are in favor of profit based on the bullish trend but limited volatility forecast by VIX as a proxy for DJIA.

We can use a variety of calculators to confirm our trades once we set them up. Using the theoretical calculators, or Greek calculators as they are commonly known, is typically less helpful than doing basic analysis of the underlying security for the option, choosing a trend, then verifying the option's potential profit through either our brokers' calculators or the simple ones mentioned here.

We will use a credit spread trade as the next example because it is one of the easier spread trades, has a relatively lower cost, incurs only modest risk, and can be nicely profitable.

There are high-risk versions of this trade, but we will use the low-risk version because that is the focus of this guide. Anyone can lose your money quickly. We are helping you build wealth with high probability, lower profit, and lower-risk trades.

Lining up a few of the tools:

Options calculator:
http://www.optionsprofitcalculator.com/

Theoretical pricing options calculators:
http://www.volatilitytrading.net/optioncalculator.htm

And my preferred simple calculator:
http://www.optionstrategist.com/calculators/probability

These calculators will help us identify our risk levels, potential profit, and general probability for profit with a particular options trade.

Google options will serve us for this trade example.

Analysis First

We have to determine what the trend is for a market or if it is trading without a trend. We will use the basic 20 and 200 EMAs (exponential moving average) compared to the S&P 500 and NASDAQ.

Source: Yahoo! Finance

We need to determine these technical factors before deciding to enter into a particular option spread:

1) What is the current trend for the underlying security? Based on the recent positive crossover above the 20 EMA and the extended time above the 200 EMA, the trend is definitely bullish. This suggests that call options, or selling puts, has a higher probability of profit, for the near term at least. I used exponential moving average because some traders prefer it and I want to show that both forms of moving averages work.

2) Are we near a possible reversal? A variety of factors, including tapering volume trends, parabolic

131

price spikes, and several other indicators can suggest a near-term reversal. Both the 20 and 200 EMA and the volume levels are indicating continued upward movement. The bullish trend is probably not near a reversal.

Choosing Directions: Our direction for the trend is up, or bullish, for GOOG, the underlying security. I used the same principles for determining a bullish trend as in the previous example. This means we can choose any of the several bullish-oriented credit spread strategies.

Choosing a Strategy

I will use the bull put credit spread. I will sell a higher-striking ITM (in-the-money) put option and buy a lower-striking OTM (out-of-the-money) put option on the GOOG options with the same expiration date.

Choosing Timeframes: Our timeframes will be relatively short in most spread trading for minimizing long-term risk and time decay, if the time decay works against us. In this case, we are using time decay to our advantage. We choose as close an expiration date as possible while achieving a sufficient premium credit. November is the closest month for expiration for this trade.

Choosing Our Strike Price: Depending on the chart volatility and volume of options available, we could go as high as we want to for assuring a low-risk trade. GOOG shows that bouncing fifty points is not unusual for a single month. That shows high volatility. We need to consider that band of volatility for our strike price selection.

We will choose a strike price of around 887, GOOG's current bid, but we have a fair margin to work with because of the volatility.

Choosing Vehicles

Based on our volatility analysis, we will sell an ITM November 13 put at 900 for $29.40. We then buy an OTM put below our sold put at 870 for $11.80. These exact strike prices were chosen carefully based on securing a safe and fungible trade, as explained below.

Watching Options Mechanics to Avoid Friction Costs

Once you choose the least expensive broker for your style of trading, there a few other ways to minimize your friction or execution costs when trading multiple options.

1) Volume - We need sufficient trading volume to avoid bumping the premium with our purchase and to be able to execute in or out of the trade without delay.

2) Premium Levels - Some options covering the same underlying security have a higher premium than others with nearby strike prices. We generally want to minimize our premiums unless we are selling the option. Either way, we want to optimize the premium for our trade.

These two criteria pushed the trade to the 900 and 870 puts because each of them had sufficient volume and open interest to execute our trade.

900.00	GOOG131101P00900000	26.40	↑5.50	24.90	26.90	7	43
900.00	GOOG7131108P00900000	34.40	0.00	26.10	29.00	5	5
900.00	GOOG131116P00900000	29.40	↑5.00	28.40	29.60	122	369
900.00	GOOG7131116P00900000	27.00	↓1.80	27.40	30.40	1	31

865.00	GOOG7131116P00865000	11.90	0.00	12.80	13.60	15	41
870.00	GOOG131101P00870000	11.80	↑1.20	11.30	12.30	109	66
870.00	GOOG7131101P00870000	15.00	0.00	9.60	12.50	2	19
870.00	GOOG131108P00870000	12.71	↑1.31	12.60	13.80	5	1
870.00	GOOG7131108P00870000	25.10	0.00	11.30	14.20	1	1
870.00	GOOG131116P00870000	15.30	↑3.10	14.50	15.20	191	384
870.00	GOOG7131116P00870000	12.70	0.00	13.60	15.30	1	61
875.00	GOOG131101P00875000	13.75	↑2.45	13.20	13.80	25	59

Source: Yahoo! Finance

Both 900 and 870 have sufficient volume and open interest for safe execution of our trade.

Calculating potential profit for our bull put spread:

Max Profit = Net Premium Received - Commissions Paid

For us to receive the maximum profit, we need the underlying price of GOOG to remain below or equal to the strike price of the long put.

Our breakeven point for our bull put spread can be calculated as follows:

Breakeven Point = Strike Price of Short Put - Net Premium Received

134

In this example, for each option pair we would receive $29.40 - $11.80 or $17.60 in credit.

Our hope is that GOOG continues rising at least moderately and exceeds the 900 level. Both options will then expire worthless by our November options expiry date. This produces the maximum profit.

If we got our trend call wrong (or GOOG announces it has decided to sell itself to AOL!), our worst-case scenario will unfold.

For example, GOOG could decline to 800 before the options expire. We are then in a situation where both options are ITM. The 870 November call is going to be worth at least $70 on an intrinsic basis, while the 900 November call will be worth $100. The spread is now $30. Having received $17.60 in credit, the loss will be $30 - $17.60 or $12.40.

Note that all calculations are based at one option, while a real trade will be based at a hundred. This means that the profit could be $1,760 or the loss could be $1240.
I will put all of this into my trading planning sheet.

Sector: Tech / Media sector. Large Cap
Sector Major Trend: Bullish
Underlying Security: GOOG

Option(s) Traded: Sell an ITM Nov '13 put at 900 for $29.40

                     Buy an OTM Nov '13 put at 870
for $11.80

135

Strategies Applied: Bull Put Credit Spread

Expected Trade Duration: Before Nov 16 expiration.

Max Loss Allowed: $1240 based on GOOG falling to $800

Triggers for Quick Close: Earnings announcement disappoints.

Potential Upside: Credit for entering the trade less commissions.

Potential Downside: Difference between the sold ITM put and the bought OTM put plus commissions.

Probability of Profit: Google has wildly swinging volatility. As of this writing, GOOG's one month volatility is 48% based on Morningstar ratings here:

http://quote.morningstar.com/Option/Options.aspx?ticker=GOOG

The probability of the price ending below 870 is: 41.5%;

The probability of the price ending above 900 is: 43.6%;

Too close to call with a slight edge toward profit. This is why I rely on the trend charts more than the probability calculators.

These two examples show how the basics are applied in two different trades. With both bullish and bearish trends, the same principles apply. All you need to do is follow the sequence and your trades will be heavily tilted toward profitability. The simpler you can keep your techniques, the less there is to screw up. You can set up trading alerts with your brokers that look for trend changes, new highs, new lows, and similar signals, but you can easily become overwhelmed with too many signals to watch and too much information to make a decision. Focusing on the few indicators that have worked for traders over the years, such as the Turtle Trend Traders, is the way to improve your odds.

7. Risk Control & Money Management - The Critical Skill

I already touched on one of the most basic concepts of risk control, that being how much of your investing capital you risk on each trade. The recommended amount is 1% to 2% risked on each trade, but that is often not a realistic amount for somebody who is starting out. If you happen to have a very large portfolio, perhaps over a hundred thousand dollars, that you are ready to risk in options trading, then the 2% level is one you can easily adhere to. If, however, you are more typical and are able to invest perhaps $10,000 in your option trading, then a 2% limit will severely restrict your trading early on.

There are some ways around this. You can trade stock option mini-contracts on exchanges, or you can trade lower-priced options.

Stock option mini-contracts are fairly new. Instead of having the typical leverage of a hundred shares per option, they control ten shares.

While that may not sound very exciting, when you're in the skill-building stage of learning how to be a successful option spread trader, you have to focus on the process and not the result. That means focusing on the basics over and over again until they're second-nature, and then winning will take care of itself.

While it may be boring, every great champion or person of notable success in a particular field or arena has had one trait in common with the others—the passion to work at the basics.

I also recommend that you start out your trading with simulation accounts. Go through all of the emotions I have outlined here in the simulated trading environment and see how well they work for you. This is one form of risk control because you are seeing how your trades can devour your investment capital when they go south. Fortunately, the trades I have focused on and explained in this guide are the type that limit your downside.

I recommend that all of the trades you engage in initially be the kinds that have a very limited downside, often restricted only to what you invested in the trade. That way you know immediately what your risk element is. The objective of option spread trading is to minimize risk by hedging your analysis of the market direction. If we all knew exactly what the market was going to do, there would be no reason to hedge or use spread trading. Since that is not the case, using option spread strategies is one of the least appreciated and best methods for you to create a part-time income from your trading capital.

The main risk control strategy is simply entering into trades where you have limited your downside, identified the percentage of your portfolio you are willing to risk, which has to be below 5%, and done your homework for pushing the odds for profit steeply in your favor. This process takes the form of analyzing the charts, being aware of potential reversal patterns or exterior events such as political and news events that could bounce you out of your trade, and making a trading plan as I have described.

Once you have set your risk tolerance bar, established your trading methodology, and adapted to the option spread strategies, you are already in a low-risk trading environment. The real issue with risk comes about when you get on only one side of the market or security. Option trading with the spread strategies I recommend prevents that problem.

Once you have gone through the process of simulated trading and feel comfortable enough to execute real trades, letting a few of your winners run will quickly build up your trading portfolio. Once you start hitting $40,000 and $50,000 in trading assets, it is wise to back off from 5% down to a 3% risk on any one trade. The message is to scale your risk with your resources.

Key Risk-Control models

In trading, there are a couple of risk-control models that can help you manage your trading account to maximize your profit potential while minimizing risk. These are equity Risk, Adjusted equity risk model, and the Total equity risk model.

Equity Risk Model

An equity risk model takes into account the level of risk you're going to take on in each trade and then calculates that risk using the amount of capital you have in your trading account.

For example, let's say you have a $30,000 trading account and that you can risk an average of 2% on each trade, putting your total risk loss at $600 for each trade. If you take an option spread position in a given stock, you'll take into account your total downside risk to be no more than $600.

Now, some spread trades may have a risk of $2,000 when your risk point is at $600. How do you compensate?

This model acts as a framework to help you make that decision. You could:

1. Take the trade but exit if the trade goes against you after hitting a $600 stop loss for the position.

2. Avoid the trade altogether.

3. Use an alternative option spread strategy to lower the risk profile.

As your trading capital increases, you can increase the level of risk you take on by following the parameters of this model. For example, once your account grows to $40,000, you can raise your risk loss to $800.

The thing that is most important when using the equity risk model is remembering to keep your level of risk limited to the amount of capital you have to trade with.

Adjusted Equity Risk Model

This risk model is for very conservative traders who don't want to experience steep drawdowns but are satisfied with lower returns in order to experience less volatility.

For example, suppose you have a $30,000 account with a 2% risk limit. You're presented with a trade opportunity but happen to have an option spread position that was already deployed. That position currently has $5,000 of your capital tied up, which leaves you with $25,000 in capital left over.

Since you are using the adjusted equity risk model, you would calculate your 2% risk against the $25,000 left over, not the original $30,000 as you would with the equity risk model.

Now you would calculate the following as:

> $25,000 in remaining trade capital x 2% risk limit = $500 risk allowed

Every trade you place will then lower the amount of money you can risk. At some point, if you have enough trades in place, you won't have enough money to risk for new trades.

There are pros and cons to using this approach, but keep in mind that this risk model is designed to keep you from becoming overleveraged.

If you're the cautious type, this is a risk model you should strongly consider, especially in the beginning.

Total Equity Risk Model

This model is for aggressive traders who like to scale up their trading and returns. I should warn you, however, that it is not for the faint of heart.

Using our previous example, if you have a $30,000 trading account and you use a 2% risk limit, your maximum risk per trade is going to be $600 ($30,000 x 2% risk limit = $600 risk per trade).

Let's say you put on an option spread position that takes $5,000 in capital to construct. After three weeks, the option spread position is now profitable by $2,500, which gives you a total equity position of $32,500 ($25,000 trade capital + $5,000 option spread position + $2,500 in profits = $32,500).

At that time, you find another trade with potential that has a total risk of $325 if the trade goes bad.

Using the total equity risk model, you calculate the following:

$32,500 in total trade equity x 2% = $650

Using this risk model, you can actually take two positions in the new opportunity you see setting up.

Can you begin to understand how much money you can make by scaling up this way?
Let me warn you again, however, that this is not for the faint of heart.

If you're a beginner, I highly advise you not to use this risk model because it can get you into trouble if you don't know what you're doing.

Even then, a "black swan" event (i.e., a 9/11 type of attack, 2008 housing bubble, blackout, system failure on Wall Street, etc.) can potentially wipe out your positions faster than you can protect them if you've overleveraged in spreads.

You need a lot of experience to work with this risk model, but once you have it, the potential is enormous.

Summing It Up

This is just a brief overview of risk control, but you now know more than 95% of option traders, which gives you a big edge.

My advice is to become a hardcore student of risk and money management. This will give you the ability to grow your account without losing a lot of sleep.

Amateurs focus on how much money they are going to make on a given trade, but the pros focus on how to lower their risk and let the money take care of itself as a result.

Start small, trade small in the beginning, and it will pay huge dividends for you later on down the line.

8. Conclusion

I already touched on one of the most basic concepts of risk control, that being how much of your investing capital you risk on each trade. The recommended amount is 1% to 2% risked on each trade, but that is often not a realistic amount for somebody who is starting out. If you happen to have a very large portfolio, perhaps over a hundred thousand dollars, that you are ready to risk in options trading, then the 2% level is one you can easily adhere to. If, however, you are more typical and are able to invest perhaps $10,000 in your option trading, then a 2% limit will severely restrict your trading early on.

There are some ways around this. You can trade stock option mini-contracts on exchanges, or you can trade lower-priced options.

Stock option mini-contracts are fairly new. Instead of having the typical leverage of a hundred shares per option, they control ten shares.

While that may not sound very exciting, when you're in the skill-building stage of learning how to be a successful option spread trader, you have to focus on the process and not the result. That means focusing on the basics over and over again until they're second-nature, and then winning will take care of itself.

While it may be boring, every great champion or person of notable success in a particular field or arena has had one trait in common with the others—the passion to work at the basics.

I also recommend that you start out your trading with simulation accounts. Go through all of the emotions I have outlined here in the simulated trading environment and see how well they work for you. This is one form of risk control because you are seeing how your trades can devour your investment capital when they go south. Fortunately, the trades I have focused on and explained in this guide are the type that limit your downside.

I recommend that all of the trades you engage in initially be the kinds that have a very limited downside, often restricted only to what you invested in the trade. That way you know immediately what your risk element is. The objective of option spread trading is to minimize risk by hedging your analysis of the market direction. If we all knew exactly what the market was going to do, there would be no reason to hedge or use spread trading. Since that is not the case, using option spread strategies is one of the least appreciated and best methods for you to create a part-time income from your trading capital.

The main risk control strategy is simply entering into trades where you have limited your downside, identified the percentage of your portfolio you are willing to risk, which has to be below 5%, and done your homework for pushing the odds for profit steeply in your favor. This process takes the form of analyzing the charts, being aware of potential reversal patterns or exterior events such as political and news events that could bounce you out of your trade, and making a trading plan as I have described.

Once you have set your risk tolerance bar, established your trading methodology, and adapted to the option spread strategies, you are already in a low-risk trading environment. The real issue with risk comes about when you get on only one side of the market or security. Option trading with the spread strategies I recommend prevents that problem.

Once you have gone through the process of simulated trading and feel comfortable enough to execute real trades, letting a few of your winners run will quickly build up your trading portfolio. Once you start hitting $40,000 and $50,000 in trading assets, it is wise to back off from 5% down to a 3% risk on any one trade. The message is to scale your risk with your resources.

Key Risk-Control models

In trading, there are a couple of risk-control models that can help you manage your trading account to maximize your profit potential while minimizing risk. These are equity Risk, Adjusted equity risk model, and the Total equity risk model.

Equity Risk Model

An equity risk model takes into account the level of risk you're going to take on in each trade and then calculates that risk using the amount of capital you have in your trading account.

For example, let's say you have a $30,000 trading account and that you can risk an average of 2% on each trade, putting your total risk loss at $600 for each trade. If you take an option spread position in a given stock, you'll take into account your total downside risk to be no more than $600.

Now, some spread trades may have a risk of $2,000 when your risk point is at $600. How do you compensate?

This model acts as a framework to help you make that decision. You could:

1. Take the trade but exit if the trade goes against you after hitting a $600 stop loss for the position.

2. Avoid the trade altogether.

3. Use an alternative option spread strategy to lower the risk profile.

As your trading capital increases, you can increase the level of risk you take on by following the parameters of this model. For example, once your account grows to $40,000, you can raise your risk loss to $800.

The thing that is most important when using the equity risk model is remembering to keep your level of risk limited to the amount of capital you have to trade with.

Adjusted Equity Risk Model

This risk model is for very conservative traders who don't want to experience steep drawdowns but are satisfied with lower returns in order to experience less volatility.

For example, suppose you have a $30,000 account with a 2% risk limit. You're presented with a trade opportunity but happen to have an option spread position that was already deployed. That position currently has $5,000 of your capital tied up, which leaves you with $25,000 in capital left over.

Since you are using the adjusted equity risk model, you would calculate your 2% risk against the $25,000 left over, not the original $30,000 as you would with the equity risk model.

Now you would calculate the following as:

> $25,000 in remaining trade capital x 2% risk limit = $500 risk allowed

Every trade you place will then lower the amount of money you can risk. At some point, if you have enough trades in place, you won't have enough money to risk for new trades.

There are pros and cons to using this approach, but keep in mind that this risk model is designed to keep you from becoming overleveraged.

If you're the cautious type, this is a risk model you should strongly consider, especially in the beginning.

Total Equity Risk Model

This model is for aggressive traders who like to scale up their trading and returns. I should warn you, however, that it is not for the faint of heart.

Using our previous example, if you have a $30,000 trading account and you use a 2% risk limit, your maximum risk per trade is going to be $600 ($30,000 x 2% risk limit = $600 risk per trade).

Let's say you put on an option spread position that takes $5,000 in capital to construct. After three weeks, the option spread position is now profitable by $2,500, which gives you a total equity position of $32,500 ($25,000 trade capital + $5,000 option spread position + $2,500 in profits = $32,500).

At that time, you find another trade with potential that has a total risk of $325 if the trade goes bad.

Using the total equity risk model, you calculate the following:

$32,500 in total trade equity x 2% = $650

Using this risk model, you can actually take two positions in the new opportunity you see setting up.

Can you begin to understand how much money you can make by scaling up this way?
Let me warn you again, however, that this is not for the faint of heart.

If you're a beginner, I highly advise you not to use this risk model because it can get you into trouble if you don't know what you're doing.

Even then, a "black swan" event (i.e., a 9/11 type of attack, 2008 housing bubble, blackout, system failure on Wall Street, etc.) can potentially wipe out your positions faster than you can protect them if you've overleveraged in spreads.

You need a lot of experience to work with this risk model, but once you have it, the potential is enormous.

Summing It Up

This is just a brief overview of risk control, but you now know more than 95% of option traders, which gives you a big edge.

My advice is to become a hardcore student of risk and money management. This will give you the ability to grow your account without losing a lot of sleep.

Amateurs focus on how much money they are going to make on a given trade, but the pros focus on how to lower their risk and let the money take care of itself as a result.

Start small, trade small in the beginning, and it will pay huge dividends for you later on down the line.

8. Conclusion

My hope in writing this guide is that you take it, learn from it, and begin trading. There are guides available for options trading that someone with a PhD in mathematics might have a hard time following, and yet those guides cannot assure you of any greater level of profitability then I can. None of the methods I have explained are unique, nor did I invent any of them. The origin of technical analysis goes back many years and even includes analyzing how the stars, sun, and moon affect the stock market. I chose to stick with more easily discerned technical patterns.

I did you the favor of trying virtually all the systems out there before I came back full circle to the simplest methodologies that seemed to work as well or better than the more complicated ones I tried. A great example of a well-known but extremely complicated trading system is the Elliott wave principle. I studied and attempted to use the Elliott wave principle only to find that even the experts had two or three variations on every wave. That level of confusion made the Elliott wave theory unworkable for me as a trading indicator.

Simply defining the trends and looking for confirmation between the short-term and long-term trend lines and occasionally volume is often more than enough to push our trading confidence above the 55% level I like to see. Even very successful traders sometimes do not trade profitably any more than 55% of the time. They are still able to make their millions, or billions in some cases, because they let their winners run.

The basic concepts for you to recognize are analyzing the market from a technical perspective for short-term trades, choosing the right strategy that matches the trend of the market, either bullish or bearish, and writing out your trade plan for what would bounce you out of the trade and how long you expect to be in it, along with your profit and loss potentials. If you follow this simple regimen as I have clearly explained it in this guide, you will be amazed at your potential for creating profitable trades on a monthly basis.

The dream of every option trader, and my goal as well when I started out, is to create a part-time income from relatively little work done by trading the markets with options. That dream is entirely within your grasp if you follow the solid principles I've laid out.

One warning for anyone who is jumping into trading for the first time: it is better not to trade then to trade without establishing the odds in your favor. I cannot emphasize enough that the hallmark of a trader who is heading down a slippery slope to losing a lot of money is that he or she overtrades. In order to trade profitably, you have to be like a sniper. You are not taking aim at every potential opportunity, but rather carefully setting yourself up to make the most of one opportunity.

In closing, I want to leave you with a few bits of advice to help you on your journey.

**There will be times when you're tempted to make a high-risk trade, and you might get away with it. Worse, you'll make a lot of money. I say "worse" because there is nothing more dangerous than doing something stupid and profiting from it. It builds bad habits.

You can run around in a dynamite factory with a lighted match and survive, but you're still an idiot for having done it.

**There is a big difference between wanting to do something and being committed to it.

If you want to be a successful option trader, you'll have to commit to becoming a success.

If you just kind of want to be an option trader, then chances are, you won't.

There is a huge distinction between wanting something and being committed to doing/becoming something. However, once you truly commit to something, you'll find that true commitment has a power and boldness that other people rarely experience.

Go for it and commit to being the best damned trader you can be.

**The worst emotion that can carry over into your trading is euphoria.

People think fear and greed are the worst, but they're not. Euphoria makes you feel like you're as good-looking as George Clooney when you really look like Danny Devito. You make a big trade and gain some serious profits, and now you begin to think you're a Wall Street icon like Warren Buffet or George Soros.

Euphoria is the crystal meth of option trading. You begin to think you're smarter than you are and that you have some kind of unique insight into the market that mere mortals don't possess.

You trade bigger and riskier until the gods of Wall Street smack you down and leave you bloody.

**Don't counter-trend trade the market when you're starting out. Save yourself a lot of sleepless nights and make life easier on yourself by trading in the direction of the trend.
Trying to catch a falling knife or time the top of the market is a futile exercise even for the pros.

You know the advertisements that say "This newsletter guru called the housing crisis…the dot-com bubble…Miley Cyrus' twerking…"?

More than likely they called those events a hundred times if they called it once (and that's a big maybe that they ever called it at all).

That stuff is guru-talk.

Trade with the trend and you'll make more money than the clowns who try to predict the future.

This brings me to…

**Be an interpreter, not a predictor.

You know how much money you'll make as a predictor in the stock market or in trading in general? None. None at all.

And you shouldn't sweat it.

Why not?

It's not your job, that's why.

Don't worry about what the market is going to do in the future. People who try to outsmart themselves by making wild predictions about future price action are overcomplicating things for themselves. Worse, they are sabotaging their own efforts.

If you find yourself saying "Hmmm. The Fed kept rates flat, and this earnings season was exceptionally positive, but unemployment remains high. That must mean there won't be much discretionary income for consumers this Christmas, so I'll start shorting Dillard's and Best Buy." And then you get creamed by the Bulls during one of the best Christmas retail seasons in the history of mankind.

Don't be a bonehead like that.

Interpret price action and look at where price is, where it came from, and what direction it's moving in. Then look for low-risk points at which to enter and exit.

I'm not saying to be mindful of a stock or market being oversold or overbought. Just plan for it and adjust your stops accordingly.

**Don't overcomplicate things for yourself.

Have you ever met someone who thinks and thinks about a problem or challenge you could solve for them in about two seconds?

They're a good person, but they just have this maddening ability to take something simple and overcomplicate the hell out of it.

This overcomplicating bias is like a virus that infects traders of every level of experience.
They'll take something simple—a trading method, a setup, an option strategy—mutate it into something that is completely unrecognizable, and render it ineffective.

Don't be that guy.

If you start to do that, take a deep breath and clear your head.

Simple equals reliable. Reliable equals proven. Proof translates into profits over time.

See how simple it is?

**Don't lose money.

If you don't have a retirement account, a 401k, a house, savings, life insurance, or simply a sound financial foundation, then maybe trading isn't for you right now.

I know it's heresy for me to say that. I mean, I just sold you this book, so what the hell?
OK, hear me out.

If you're down to your last two grand, $200,000 in credit card debt, forty-six years old with no retirement plan, and you've got a family, then how mentally/emotionally stable do you think you're going to be when trading away at that $2,000?

Now, you could be a complete freak with iron discipline and a mindset for success to rival that of King Solomon, but most people aren't.

Losing money can become a habit.

If you build your financial house on a firm foundation, you'll be more aware of risk because you know how hard it is to make a buck and invest it. Better, you trade with a much better state of mind.

Most people (myself included) need a measure of stability and security to fall back on in order to take on the level of risk that comes with speculation.

Your trading account should ideally make up no more than 5% to 10% of your total net worth. Most financial advisors would allocate that much of your investment portfolio to high-risk/high-reward investments. You'll be ahead of the curve by taking control of that portion of your portfolio and trading it yourself.

Don't be afraid to take a personal and financial inventory and begin building that foundation. And if you've got a family, for Chrissake, you owe it to them to do so.

OK, if you've read this far then you're serious about success in trading, and I want to wish you the best of luck.

Few things can hold a person back who has the right combination of grit, tenacity, intelligence, discipline, and the will to keep going forward.

If there's anything I can do to help you, drop me a line through my site: www.stockoptionsystem.com.

Good trading.

Made in the USA
Middletown, DE
18 June 2016